# OPTIONS TRADING FOR BEGINNERS
# CRASH COURSE

LEARN THE STRATEGIES & TECHNIQUES TO MAKE MONEY IN FEW WEEKS
GENERATING REGULAR, CONSISTENT PASSIVE INCOME IN THE STOCK MARKET
WITHOUT TAKING BIG RISK

# Contents

**Title Page**
**Contents**
**Copyright**
**Introduction**
**1. Options Basics**
**2. Basic Terms of Options Trading**
**3. Getting Started with Options Trading**
**4. Strategies for Options Trading**
**5. Strategies for New Options Traders**
**Afterword**

# INTRODUCTION

The use of options is one of the most successful trading strategies accessible to traders today. They provide traders with the opportunity to leverage positions, control risk, and increase the profits on their current portfolios, among other things. This book gives the practical knowledge—from fundamental ideas to complex techniques—required for successful options trading to those who desire to do so. Its purpose is to provide trading tactics to both rookie and intermediate traders. As options traders, we must concentrate on the many events that can cause markets to move in one of three dimensions up, down, or sideways. Paying careful attention to volatility is one of the most important things that must become a part of your everyday market strategy if you want to succeed in the market. How quickly can a single incident move the markets, and what strategies can we use to take advantage of this event? When historical and implied volatility vary, what techniques may mitigate the situation? Options give the experienced investor or trader the ability to construct situations that others may not anticipate or predict. Unlike a stock investor, who can only buy or sell one stock, an options trader may use various techniques for a variety of different time periods. In the same manner, once you have mastered a couple or more of these tactics, you will be able to use them time and time again for the rest of your trading career. Some tactics, for example, enable you to benefit from the directional movement of a stock without actually purchasing the stock, all while taking on far less risk than if you had purchased the stock directly.

It is possible to safeguard your portfolio against the next market crisis by using other tactics, similar to purchasing insurance for your portfolio. On the other hand, other tactics enable you to receive "income" consistently. As a result, an "option" is a solution to the challenges that many novice traders have when entering the world of stock trading. However, most new participants lack the confidence to invest in stocks and choose to start with something more secure. A standard store's "options" section allows you to do much more than that, enabling you to bet on a changing stock index while being protected from the market and therefore protecting yourself in the event of a market collapse. As a result, investing in stocks is a secure investment that will help you avoid market hazards.

If you finish this book, you will have a fundamental understanding of the trade. You may even study more and begin practicing to understand the ins and outs of the industry. Remember that all of those great traders out there did not start that way; it has taken them years of experience to get to where they are now. Although it may seem a little intimidating at first, if you use the proper tactics, you will have a good chance of making it big in the world of stock trading.

CHAPTER 1

# OPTIONS BASICS

An options contract is specialized in providing and selling specified stock trading quantities at a defined price inside a specific trading period before the expiration date.

# 1.1 What are Options

A contract involving two parties based on relational assets is known as an option. You may build an option contract for any asset, but we'll focus on stock options contracts. Because one party to the transaction will have the opportunity to purchase or sell stocks based on whether or not specific criteria are satisfied, they are referred to as options.

A derivative is a sort of option. Even though derivatives have been around for a long time, the general public was not aware of them until the 2008 financial meltdown, when a specific sort of derivative, mortgage-backed securities, wreaked financial chaos when a large number of bets went bad at the same time. A derivative may seem sophisticated, but it simply refers to an asset whose value is evaluated based on another asset. In the scenario of options, the contract's value is determined by the value of the equities on which it is based.

One hundred shares of stock are represented by one option contract. The arrangement will cost the buyer a fraction of what that would cost to purchase stock. An options contract is essentially a wager that the stock will develop in a specified direction over a set period. As a result, they may be utilized to speculate. An options contract, like other contracts, has an expiry date or "expiry."

Options give a lot of leverage, and trading options correctly may be less dangerous than investing the actual stocks directly, as provided as you don't misuse it.

# 1.2 Types of Options

Based on whether you're buying or selling, you have two choices:

### 1.1.1 Call Options

Call options are contracts that allow investors the right to acquire 100 shares of stock over a certain time period. Investors will purchase call options if they feel the value of a stock or investment will rise. They may benefit from the higher value when they eventually sell the shares by purchasing these options at a preset price.

### 1.1.2 Put Options

Put options are the polar opposite of call options in that they enable investors to sell a certain number of shares over a specific time period. Because of this discrepancy, investors usually hope for a greater price in order to benefit since this indicates a better value for the option. Essentially, you want to have the item's value or shares fall when you purchase put options.

### 1.1.3 Styles of Options

Although the qualities of the American and European alternatives are similar, the variances are significant. Owners of American-style options, for example, may exercise their options at any moment before they expire. On the other hand, European-style options may only be exercised when they reach their expiry date.

## 1.3 Practical Examples

**Put options**

A put option is a contractual relationship to swap a stock at a set strike price by a certain date. One party, the put buyer, has the right but not the responsibility to sell the shares at the striking price by a certain date in the future. The put seller's second party is obligated to purchase the stock from the put buyer at the strike price if the buyer performs the option.

For instance, if a company is priced at $50 and you believe it will fall to $40, you may purchase a $45 put option for $0.20. If the stock drops to $40, you may sell it for $45, making a profit of $4.80 per share. The investor who sold you the put, on the other hand, would be compelled to purchase the shares from you at $45, a loss of $4.80. The option expires worthless if the stock never falls below $45 by the expiry date, and the put buyer loses $0.20 while the put seller retains the $0.20.

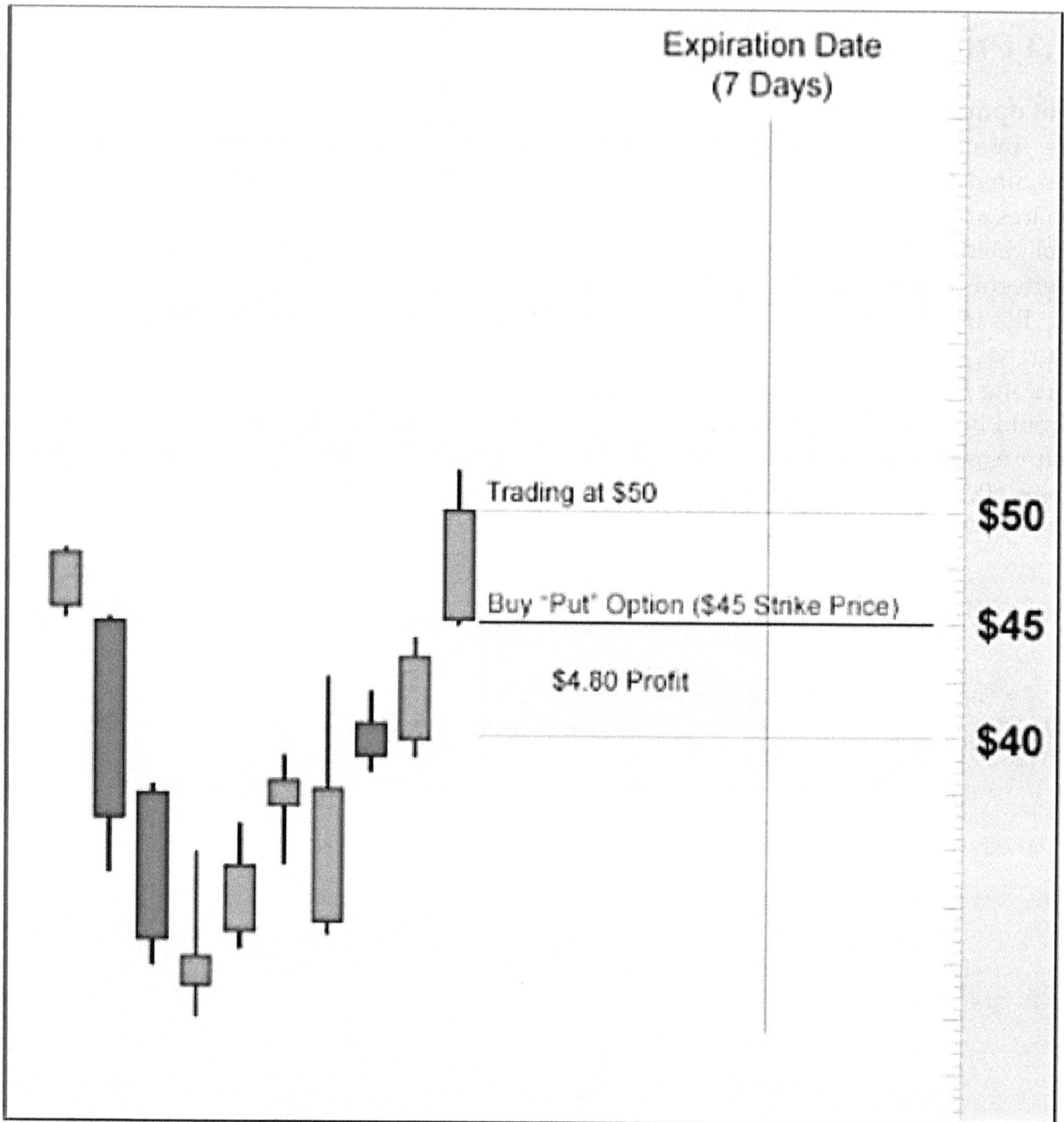

Expiration Date
(7 Days)

Trading at $50

Buy "Put" Option ($45 Strike Price)

$4.80 Profit

$50

$45

$40

## Call Options

A call option is a contractual relationship to swap a stock at a set strike price by a certain date. The buyer of the call has the entitlement, but not the duty, to purchase the stock at the strike price by another date in the future. The seller of the call, on the other hand, is obligated to sell the shares to the bidder at the striking price if the option is exercised.

For illustration, if a stock is priced at $50 and you believe it will rise to $60, you may purchase a $55 call option for $0.20. If the stock increased to $60, you could purchase it for $55, even if it is worth $60, making a $4.80 profit on each share. The individual who sold you the call, on the other hand, would be compelled to sell you the shares at $55, a loss of $4.80. If the stock does not climb over $55 by the expiry date, the call becomes worthless, and the call buyer loses $0.20 while the call seller retains $0.20.

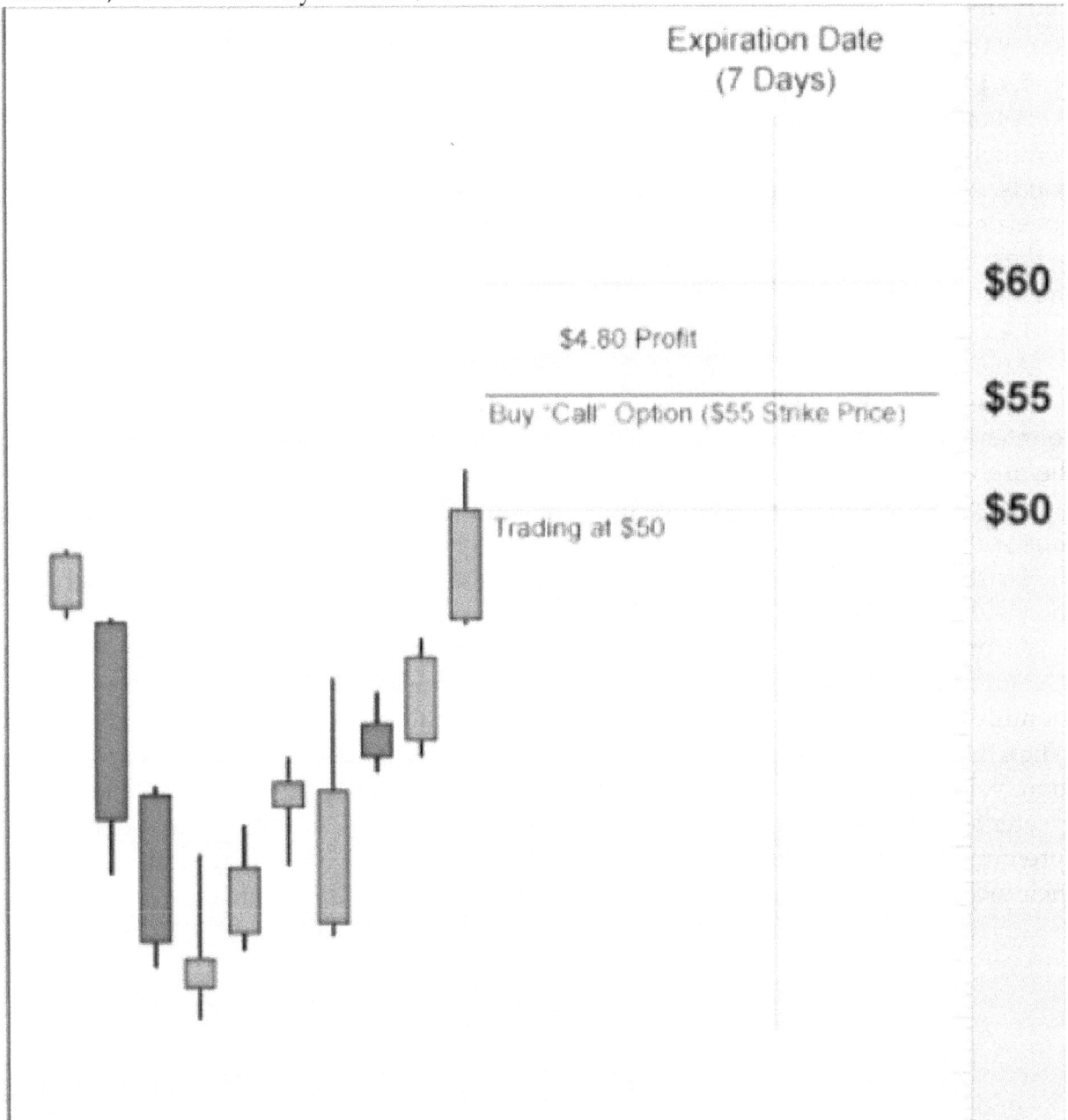

Expiration Date
(7 Days)

$60

$4.80 Profit

Buy "Call" Option ($55 Strike Price)

$55

Trading at $50

$50

# 1.4 Bond Options

An opportunity to expand with a bond as the entire product is known as a bond option. Like other conventional option contracts, bond call and bond put options allow an investor to take a variety of speculative positions. All forms of options, notably bond options, are derivatives that enable investors to make speculative wagers on the trend of underpinning equity prices or hedge specific value risks within a portfolio.

### 1.4.1 What Makes Bond a Bond?

A bond is a debt instrument made to the bond issuer by the bond consumer or bondholder. When governments, businesses, and municipalities want funds, they issue bonds. An investor who purchases a government bond effectively lends money to the government. When an investor purchases a corporate bond, they effectively lend money to the company. A bond, like a loan, pays interest regularly and repays the principal at the maturity date.

### 1.4.2 Determine the Price of Bond in the Market

After they are issued, bonds may be purchased and sold in the "secondary market." While some bonds are transacted on exchanges, the majority are exchanged over the counter between huge broker-dealers operating on behalf of their customers or themselves.

The secondary market value of a bond is determined by its price and yield. A bond must, of course, have a cost at which it can be purchased and sold, and a bond's yield is the yearly return an investor may anticipate if the bond is held until maturity. As a result, the yield is calculated using the bond's purchase price and the coupon.

As previously shown, the bond price always changes the direction of its yield. Recognize that a bond's price represents the magnitude of the income it generates via its monthly coupon interest payments to grasp this crucial characteristic of the bond market. When interest rates fall, especially on government bonds, older bonds of all sorts become more valuable since they were sold when interest rates were higher and hence had greater coupons. To sell older bonds in the secondary market, investors might demand a "premium." On the other hand, older bonds may lose value if interest rates increase since their yields are significantly small, and older bonds sell at a "discount."

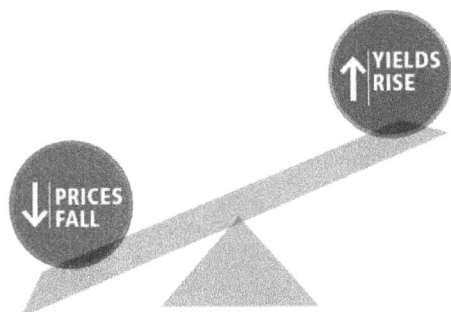
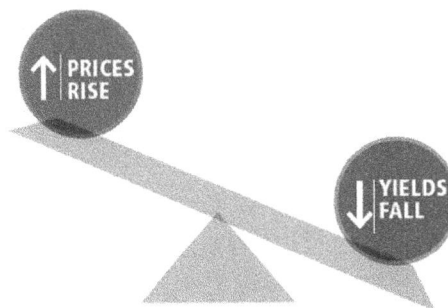

### Example

Let's say a company wants to invest $1 million in a new manufacturing facility and chooses to make a bond offering to help pay for it. The business may elect to offer 1,000 bonds for $1,000 apiece to investors. Each bond has a $1,000 "face value" in this example. The business – now known as the bond issuer – selects a yearly interest rate, termed as the coupon, as well as a time limit for repaying the principal, or $1 million. When determining the coupon, the issuer considers the current interest rate environment, ensuring that it is reasonable with similar bonds and appealing to investors. The issuer can offer five-year bonds with a 5% yearly coupon. The bond matures after five years, at which point the firm repays each bondholder $1,000 in face value. The average time it takes to mature may significantly impact the risk and possible return an investor can anticipate. Because many more things might negatively influence the issuer's capacity to pay creditors over a 30-year term than over 5 years, a $1 million bond due in five years is often seen as less risky than a $1 million bond payable over 30 years. A longer-maturity bond's added risk is proportional to the interest rate or coupon that the issuer should collect on the bond. In other words, for a long-term bond, an issuer will pay a higher interest rate. Longer-term bonds may provide higher yields, but the investor takes on more risk in compensation for that income.

### 1.4.3 Pros and Cons of Bond Options

Incorporating bond options in your portfolio has both advantages and disadvantages.

### Pros of Bond Options

### Higher Return Potential

As seen in the example above, a bond options strategy may boost a trader's profits on a certain investment when properly performed. Bond choices might also safeguard you from losing money. Investors often use bond options as a hedge against more risky investing techniques.

### Bond Options Provide Risk Hedging

Using derivative contracts, investors may profit from interest rates and other short-term drivers of investment performance. Bond options may also be used to take advantage of price differences in options or position portfolios ahead of key geopolitical events such as presidential elections, potentially significant Federal Reserve policy decisions, large recessions, and other strong economic pressures.

## Cons of Bond Options
### Non-exercise risk
Bond option investors would be better off letting an options contract terminate than executing a deal that goes wrong and costs them money. While a bond options investor is not required to exercise their contracts, failing to do so means that the money used to acquire or sell the bond option is lost permanently. The costs that financial firms charge for processing options trading are similar.

### The Danger of Permanent Investment Loss
While call options allow an investor to make an unlimited profit if the asset appreciates, placing a call or put option exposes the investor to an unlimited risk of loss. If the underlying assets lose their value, the options investor might lose a lot of money.

### The Danger of Losing a Large Sum of Money Quickly
Due to the nature of options as short-term investment vehicles, investors must thoroughly understand approaching investment price swings to reduce the negative ability to invest in bond options. Traders often base their options strategy selections on a limited time horizon. That implies that all options traders must master two major trading objectives: understanding when to buy and when to sell an options contract or to cut losses by letting the contract terminate without invoking the option to buy or sell before the expiry date.

### 1.4.4 Types of Bond Options
Bond options provide investors the opportunity to purchase or sell (through calls and puts) a based on investment asset at a predetermined time and price.

### Bonds with a Call Option
If the underlying bond option's price increases, the contract holder may profit on the call by exercising the option to acquire the asset (using a call option) at a lower price and then releasing it when the underlying asset's price rises. If the strike price of a call option is less than the dominant position in the underlying bond, the option is in the money.

## Put Options on Bonds

A put option or placed bond is purchased by a bond options client who expects the price of a bond will rise. Buy the asset at its current low price and sell it at the increasing strike price, providing the market rises in the trader's desired direction. Being on the wrong side of an options trade, i.e., selling below market rate or buying above market rate, is something a bond investor tries to avoid.

A put option would be purchased by an investor who believes bond prices would fall in the future due to projected market circumstances. A bond put option grants the contract holder the opportunity to sell the extended warranty at the special price of $900 – on or before the expiry date – if the underlying bond option's level value is $1,000. The fundamental bond is now worth $870 if bond prices decrease. Even if the bond's value has decreased to $870, that bond option investor may now sell the options at the strike price of $900. Given the overinflated aspect of options contracts, this ensures a large reward for the investor.

### Options for Embedded Bonds

Attached bond options are bonds that provide the holder or issuer the right to perform a certain action at a specific time in the future. Call, adjustable, and grounded floating-rate clauses are examples of embedded bond options.

### 1.4.6 Options on Callable Bonds

One sort of embedded bond option is callable bonds. The issuer of callable bonds has the option of repaying investors the bond's face value before the end of the term.

# 1.5 Commodity Options

The purchasing and exchanging of these basic resources are known as commodities trading. It sometimes involves the actual exchange of items. However, futures contracts, in which you commit to purchase or sell a commodity for a specific price at a specific date, are increasingly common.

Market participants often use futures contracts to speculate on how much the value of a product will change in the future. If you feel the price will climb, you will acquire futures or go long on the stock. When you feel the price will decline, you trade futures or go bearish on the stock. While futures contracts may be used to speculate on price fluctuations, they're more often utilized by producers or significant industrial users as a protection against price, as we'll see later. Commodity exchanges are where most futures contracts are transacted.

### 1.5.1 Call Options in Commodity Trading

On the contract's expiration date, the owner of a call option has the right to purchase the inherent commodity futures at a set price or the striking price. An option buyer is said to go long on the option. If the buyer decides to exploit his right to purchase, the options contract devolves into a futures contract on the expiration date.

When a buyer of a call option sees intrinsic value, that is, when the strike price is below than price of the commodities futures contract, he will exercise his right.

### 1.5.2 How Commodity Call Options does Works

Assume trader G is pessimistic on one-month gold futures, which are now trading at Rs.1500 per lot, and expects to underlie prices to decline. He buys a one-month Gold Call Option for Rs.1150 at a mutually negotiated strike price. For the options contract, he pays a premium of Rs. 50 to the underwriter.

Trader G discovers that his bets have paid off on the contract's expiration date. Because G prefers to buy cheap, if the current price of the 1-month gold futures goes anyplace over Rs.1150, say Rs.1350 per lot, trader G will exercise his purchasing rights and convert the options to a one-month futures contract at the strike price, earning Rs.200. When the strike cost of equity of an option is cheaper than average current market pricing, the buyer is considered to be In the Money. In this case, the option's underwriter will be obligated to honor the contract.

In a different market situation, if the exchange rate of one-month gold futures is trading even fairly lower than the strike price of Rs.1150, say at Rs. 1000, the option buyer might choose not to exercise his right to purchase at the strike price. Without being exercised, the contract would expire worthlessly. Trader G would only lose the premium he paid to the underwriter.

### 1.5.3 Commodity Put Option

A commodity put option offers the holder the right to sell intrinsic commodity futures at a certain price when the term ends on a specific date, usually's final Thursday of the month.

One may also sell or guarantee a put option on commodities futures, which exposes the underwriter to price risks. If the buyer elects to invoke his right to purchase the underpinning contract, the underwriter must honor his end of the bargain. However, the underwriters' incentive comes from their premium on put option commodities transactions. Most options contracts will expire worthless if the strike price is greater than current prices on the expiration date.

### 1.5.4 How Commodity Call Options does Works

Assume trader H is positive on one-month gold futures prices and believes they will climb further from present levels of Rs.1500 per lot. Upon paying more money to the underwriter, he may purchase a one-month gold put option with a strike price of Rs.1700. The option buyer will always try to book the extended warranty at a strike price greater than his market expectations.

Much to the delight of trader H, one month only after the contract was signed, the trader discovers that one-month futures are now trading at Rs.1650. Then he'd use his authority to sell the underpinning one-month gold obligations at the strike price of Rs.1700 and bag a profit of Rs. 50 above the current market price of the futures, which is the intrinsic value. When the strike price is greater than the typical standard price and the intrinsic value is larger than zero, the trader is considered the money on the put option.

But what if the markets become extremely optimistic, and trader H discovers one-month gold futures trading at prices much higher than the strike price, say Rs.1750, on the day of options expiry? In such an instance, trader H has the choice of not exercising his put option or exercising his right to sell the overarching one-month gold prospects at the strike price of Rs.1700, resulting in a notional loss of Rs.50. The owner minimized his losses by not undertaking his right to sell. He merely loses the amount of the premium.

### 1.5.5 Types of Commodities

Commodities are lumped on as an investment product. However, there are other commodities in which you may invest. Commodities are divided into two categories: hard commodities and soft commodities. Soft commodities are cultivated or created, while hard commodities are often derived from natural resources.

### Agricultural Commodities

Farmers create soft and agricultural commodities. Agricultural commodities are rice, wheat, barley, oats, oranges, coffee beans, cotton, sugar, and cocoa. Lumber may also be classified as an agricultural commodity.

Seasonal variations, weather patterns, and climatic variables significantly impact this industry. Other variables, such as a virus that affects cattle or pork, might also have a role. If demand for specific items grows or declines, population expansion or reduction in a certain region might affect investment potential.

## Commodities for Livestock and Meat

Livestock and meat are categorized in the commodities market. Pork bellies, live cattle, poultry, live pigs, and feeder cattle are illustrations of livestock and meat commodities. These are sometimes referred to as "soft commodities."

Seasonal elements and weather patterns may not seem to have an impact on this market, but livestock and the consistent production of meat need the constant intake of feed, which is often maize or grain-based. As a result, this industry can be susceptible in unforeseen ways.

## Commodities of Energy

Commodities of energy are hard commodities. Crude oil, natural gas, heating oil, propane, and petroleum-based products like gasoline are examples of energy commodities.

Investors should be mindful of certain economic and political issues that might impact oil and gas output, such as a shift in OPEC policy. Emerging technology that supports innovative or green sources of power has the potential to have a significant influence on energy commodity pricing.

## Precious and Industrial Metals

Metals are both precious and industrial metals, and they are both hard commodities. Mining stocks such as gold, silver, and platinum are examples of metal commodities. Steel, copper, zinc, iron, and lead are industrial metals that fall within this group.

Investors should be mindful of variables such as inflation, which may lead to purchasing precious metals as a hedge.

## 1.5.6 How to Invest in Commodities

If you want to meet market demand commodities, you may do it in various ways. It's critical to comprehend the danger as well as your aims. You may use it as a starting point for deciding how most of your assets to put into commodity trading, as well as which of the following techniques to pursue.

## Trading Commodities Stocks

If you're already experienced with stock trading, acquiring shares of firms with a commodities link might be the most straightforward method to start investing.

You might, for example, invest in biotech, pesticide, or meat production firms if you want to acquire leverage to primary crops or livestock and meat commodities.

If you're more interested in energy stocks and precious or types of technological commodities markets, you could want to look into buying oil or mining stocks.

Commodity stock trading is similar to stock trading in general. The distinction is that you're focusing on firms that are in some way connected to the commodity markets. This necessitates an awareness of the company's potential as well as the effect of commodity price variations.

For even greater buying power, you may trade commodities stocks on margin. This entails lending from your brokerage and repaying it. Though a dip in stock prices might cause a margin call, this could contribute to higher earnings.

## Commodity Futures Trading

A futures contract is a contract to purchase or sell almost any commodity at a price at a specific date in the future. Commodity futures contracts are made available to investors by raw material producers.

An orange producer, for example, may acquire a futures contract committing to sell a particular quantity of their harvest for a certain price. A firm that sells orange juice may then obtain the contract to buy those oranges at that production price.

The exchange of tangible commodities or raw materials occurs in this sort of futures trading. Futures trading in commodities does not usually imply that you intend to take delivery of two tonnes of coffee beans or 4,000 bushels of maize to the average investor. Rather, you purchase a futures contract to sell it before the term ends.

Commodity futures trading is speculative because investors speculate on how a commodity's price will fluctuate in the future. Commodities futures may be traded on margin in the same way commodities stocks can. However, if the product's price does not move in the direction you anticipate, this might imply taking on additional risk.

Commodity ETFs (or exchange-traded funds) may help you trade commodities more efficiently. You are purchasing a basket of assets when you buy a commodities ETF. These may be tailored to a specific commodity, such as metals or energy, or they might provide exposure to the whole commodities market.

Commodity exchange-traded funds (ETFs) may simplify diversification, but knowing what you're investing in is crucial. For example, a commodities ETF that incorporates options or futures contracts may be riskier than an ETF that invests in commodities firms like oil and gas corporations or food producers.

## Investing in Commodities through Mutual and Index Funds

Commodities may be purchased through mutual and index funds. Mutual funds and index funds, like ETFs, may help you diversify your portfolio by allowing you to purchase a basket of commodity assets. However, compared to index funds, controlled mutual funds have access to a wide range of strategies.

Actively managed funds use an active management technique, with a portfolio manager selecting specific stocks for the fund. Investing in a commodities mutual fund focused on water or corn, for example, might expose you to a variety of firms that develop methods or equipment for water sustainability or corn production.

On the other hand, index mutual funds are passive, replicating the effectiveness of macroeconomic variables.

Even if you may invest in a portfolio of diverse assets via these funds, keep in mind that commodities mutual funds and index funds are still conceptual, so it's critical to consider the risk profile of the fund's fundamental holdings.

# 1.6 Commodity Trading Basics Beginner Must Know

No question establishing a good commodities trading strategy requires extensive study and timely analysis. Before you commence, you should be acquainted with several fundamental principles of commodities trading.

### 1.6.1 Commodity Trading is Seasonal

Commodity markets are considerably more closely tied to producers and consumers than stock markets, and as a result, commodity trading is quite cyclical. The harvesting cycle determines the availability of soft commodities such as maize and wheat. Commodity demand, including oil and gas, tends to grow in the autumn as we approach winter and decline in the spring as we approach summer.

### 1.6.2 Learn and Follow Market Trends

When trading commodities, it's extremely important to understand and follow bull and bear market patterns. The saying "the trend is your friend" is prevalent among commodities traders for a reason. To see if the market is constructive (prices increasing) or adverse (prices dropping), it is typically wiser to bet with the trend (prices falling). Of course, no trend lasts forever, so knowing the psychology and activity of the market will help you determine what to do in response to the trend.

### 1.6.3 Take the time to Identify Your Specialty

Commodity trading lends itself to specialized markets. Therefore, most experienced traders prefer to specialize in a single commodity or specialty. For example, this argument becomes evident when you examine diverse commodities like bullion and grain.

Various market movements and other factors will influence these commodities' pricing. Instead of comprehending numerous markets, it is preferable to concentrate on one. That way, you'll be able to comprehend your odds of success and learn how to improve them.

## 1.7 Currency Options

A CURRENCY Derivative is a contract mechanism used to hedge against risks associated with possibly unfavorable changes in the value of a currency pair. It also allows customers to benefit from favorable changes in the foreign exchange market. When a customer purchases CURRENCY OPTIONS, they have the opportunity to buy or sell a certain currency at a pre-determined exchange rate on a future date. The currency option buyer provides the seller with payments for a specified to gain this option.

These are non-linear instruments that market players employ for both hedging and speculation. The buyer of a Currency Option has the right, but not the responsibility, to exercise the option and get the liberty; the buyer pays the Seller/Option writer a premium.

## Currency Options

Bought a 3-month USD call INR put option on $ 2 million ── **Buyer** / **Seller** ── Sold a 3-month USD put INR call option on $ 1 million

Currency Options to buy and sell currency pair at a pre-specified price (Also known as Strike Price)

### 1.7.1 Types of Currency Options
There are two types of currency options
- Call Options
- Put Options

### Currency Call Options
A currency call options contract offers the buyer the ability to possess a foreign currency at a stated price for a set length of time. Companies purchase call options even though they believe the underlying currency's spot rate will rise. Trading currency options may be used for hedging or speculating.

## Hedging

Multinational corporations may use currency call options with available holdings in foreign currencies to hedge their positions. Consider when an American corporation purchases industrial equipment from an Indian company and pays Indian rupees upon shipment. The rate at which a US corporation may acquire Indian rupees for dollars is missing from an Indian rupee call option. Before the settlement date, such a swap between the functional currencies at the stated strike price may occur. As a result, the call option defines the American corporation's maximum price to get Rupees. If the spot price breaks under the strike price before the delivery date, the merchant may pay for its goods by purchasing Rupees at the current market rate and letting the call option expire.

## Speculation

Firms and individuals sometimes use currency call options to speculate on exchange rate variations for a certain currency. Call option speculation aims to benefit from exchange rate fluctuations by directly taking an unregulated holding. If a speculator believes that a currency's future spot rate will rise, he will engage in the following transactions:

- Purchase currency call options.
- Wait for a little longer until the currency's spot rate has risen enough.
- Purchase the currency at the strike price to exercise his option.
- At the current spot rate, sell the currency.

## Currency Put Options

A currency put option is a compact that allows the holder the authority to sell a foreign currency at a certain price over a set period. People purchase currency put options because they believe the underlying currency's spot rate will fall. Multinational corporations may use currency put options to cover open holdings in foreign currencies. Consider the case of an Indian corporation that has sold an aircraft to a Japanese company and agreed to be paid in Japanese yen. The manufacturer may be apprehensive about the risk that the yen would decline before the payment from the consumer is due. The exporter might acquire yen put options to insulate itself against currency depreciation, allowing it to sell yen at the set strike price. In effect, the exporter would lock in the lowest exchange rate where it just could sell Japanese yen for US dollars over a given period. If the yen gains over this period, on the other hand, the exporter might let the put options mature and sell the yen at the current spot rate.

Individuals may wager via currency put options by predicting exchange rate variations for a certain currency. Speculators who anticipate the Euro will devalue in the future, for example, may purchase euro put options, which allow them to sell euros at a specific strike price. They may acquire euros at the spot rate and execute their put options by selling them at the strike price if the Euro's spot rate depreciates as projected. Gamblers do not need to execute their put options to earn a profit. They might benefit by selling put options since put option premiums grow and decrease with the underlying currency's exchange rate. The seller of put options must acquire the specified currency from the owner who activates the put option at the strike price. Speculators may sell their put options if they believe the currency will appreciate. However, if the currency gains during the term, the put option will not be used. If they anticipate the currency to decline, on the other hand, they will hold their put options. When put option premiums rise, they will sell their put options.

## 1.7.2 Advantages and Disadvantages

### Advantages

- It allows traders to leverage trades since the top quality cost of the option contract is comparatively cheap compared to the cost of actually purchasing the contract, allowing them to take a huge position for a little premium.
- Corporations may employ a low-cost hedging strategy to protect themselves against unfavorable currency movements.

### Disadvantages

- Currency Options are vulnerable to exploitation by fraudsters and monopolies due to their high leverage.
- The local government of each nation controls the currency markets, which affects the price of currency options.

# 1.8 Index Options

An index paid by the consumer's derivative allows the holder to purchase or sell the volume of a market instrument, such as the S&P 500 index, at the set exercise price. There are no real stocks purchased or traded. An index option's underlying asset is often an index futures contract.

Index options are always revenue and are primarily European-style options, which means they only settle on the maturity date and do not allow for early exercise.

### 1.8.1 How Index Options Work

There are no real equities exchanged with index options since the quantitative research approach is the one that is referenced. Index futures contracts are often used as the underlying asset in index options. The underlying index cannot be physically delivered. Hence settlement is done via cash payments. Index options are European-style alternatives that are only settled at the expiry date. There is no workout in the morning. An index call option enables you to buy the index, while a put option allows you to sell the index.

Index option derivatives are moderate products that profit from an index's directional fluctuations. The upside profit potential of an index call option is infinite, while the downside loss is constrained to the price paid for the call option. The profit potential of index put options is restricted at the index's level, less the put excess paid, while the downside is constrained to the put premium.

On most indices and exchanges, index options come with a multiplier that defines the total contract price, generally 100. The opportunity to suffer minimal losses while receiving exposure to a basket of equities at a fraction of the cost is one of the most attractive features of index options.

In most circumstances, it is in the investor's best interest to lock in any profits acquired to safeguard the portfolio against a collapse beyond a set floor price. It is possible to purchase a put option contract on each index holdings to lock in a certain selling price for each company. A tiny portfolio may benefit from such a strategy, which preserves it in the case of a market crisis. However, if the inventory is broad and diverse, ensuring each position in this manner is not cost-effective.

As a result, index options are utilized to hedge the total portfolio position in big, diversified portfolios. It is accomplished by identifying the appropriate index to utilize as a portfolio proxy. The next stage is to determine the number of index options to utilize as a portfolio hedge.

### Example

Consider the case of Index X, a hypothetical index with a present level of 500. Consider the case where an investor chooses to buy a call option on Index X with a strike price of 505. If this 505 call option costs $11, the exclusive contract will cost $1,100, or $11 multiplied by 100.

It's vital to understand that the asset class in this contract is the cash level of the index modified by the multiplier, not any specific stock or collection of companies. It's $50,000 in this case or $500 multiplied by $100. An investor may purchase the option for $1,100 rather than investing $50,000 in the index's equities and use the remaining $48,900 appropriately.

This trade has a maximum risk of $1,100. The strike price plus the stated amount is the break-even point for an index call option transaction. That's 516 in this case, or 505 plus 11. This specific trade gets lucrative at any level over 516.

If the index level at expiry is 530, the call option owner would exercise it and get $2,500 in cash from the opposing side of the deal, or (530 – 505) x $100. This deal makes a profit of $1,400 after deducting the original price.

### 1.8.2 Target Group for Index Options

Investors who can suffer a capital loss and have an adequate understanding of (similar) financial products will likely employ index options. Often Investors that invest in the items have a limited investment perspective (shorter than five years). Certain index options are seen to be riskier than others. The risk indicator for a certain product may be found in the Key Shareholder Document (KID). A KID should be assigned to each index option. This is a three-page document that details the product's qualities as well as the hazards linked with it. Aside from the KID, the exchange website typically includes information on contract parameters and the underlying. Its symbol refers to the underlying of an option.

### 1.8.3 Risk and Rewards

Investing may be beneficial, but there are risks involved. Like all other financial instruments, investing in index options has the risk of loss. The maximum loss in a margin account in a put or call option is the premium you budgeted. The maximum profit on a short position in an option is the premium you earned when disposing of (writing) the option. It doesn't matter whether it's a call or a put option. And from the other hand, the most significant loss varies. A call option short position has an infinite risk of loss. The exercise price less the received premium is the maximum loss for a short position in a put option.

# 1.9 Stock Options

Stock options are a kind of reward. Employees, contractors, consultants, and investors may all get them. These contracts enable the employees the authority to purchase or exercise a pre-determined number of shares of company stock at a pre-determined price, known colloquially as the grant price. However, this deal is only valid for a limited time. Before your options expire, you have a certain timescale to exploit them. Your employer may also compel you to trigger your options within a certain amount of time after you leave.

The number of alternatives available to its workers varies depending on the firm. It will also be determined by the employee's seniority and specific talents. Investors and other stakeholders must approve off before any employee may get stock options.

### 1.9.1 How to Exercise Stock Options

You'll be able to exercise your choices after they've expired. This implies you can purchase stock in the firm. Your alternatives have no real worth unless you exercise them.

The cost of such choices is specified in the contract you executed after it first began. However, this cost is the grant price, strike price, or exercise price. This valuation will not change the fundamentals of how successfully (or badly) the firm performs.

Let's imagine you've been with the company for four years and now have 20,000 stock options with a $1 exercise price. You would need to spend $20,000 (20,000 x $1) to exercise all of your options. You already have most of the stock after you've exercised your option, and you may sell it at any time. You might also keep it and wait for a further increase in the stock price. You will also be responsible for any commissions, fees, or taxes associated with performing and transferring your options.

There are also other methods to exercise without spending the money to purchase all of your selections. You may, for example, engage in an exercise-and-sell transaction. To do so, you'll buy your options and then sell them right away. Rather than having to pay for the exercise with your own money, the brokerage managing the sale will essentially earn you the extra income by using proceeds from the sale to cover the cost of the shares.

The exercise-and-sell-to-cover transaction is another approach to exercise. You sell enough stock to pay your stock purchase and keep the remainder with this method.

Finally, you should be aware that your selections have an expiry date. This information may be found in your contract. Options typically terminate ten years from the date of award or 90 days afterward you change jobs.

There are two types of stock options.

The call option holder may purchase an asset at a certain price within a specified term.

Put options enable the hoping to send an asset at a predetermined price within a given period.

There are two types of styles available: American and European. Between both the transaction and expiry dates, American options may be activated at any time. European options, which are much less uncommon, may only be used before they expire.

### 1.9.2 When do You Exercise Your Stock Options

A variety of variables will influence when and how you exercise your stock options. First, you should probably wait until the firm goes public if it does. If you don't wait and your firm doesn't go public, your ownership may be worthless – or perhaps nothing.

Second, you'll want to activate your options only when the stock's market price climbs above your exercise price after your company's initial public offering (IPO). Consider the following scenario: your exercise price is $2 per share. When the spot price is $1, it's not a good idea to trigger your options right away. You'd be better off purchasing on the open market.

If the market price is $3 per share, on the other hand, you will profit by exercising your options and selling. However, if the price is rising, you may want to hold off on completing your options. Your money is buried in those shares once you exercise them. So why not hold off on selling till the spot price is where you want to be? You'll be able to purchase and sell without losing money for a long time if you do it this way.

However, if all factors indicate a rising stock price and you can sustain to retain your holdings for at minimum a year, you may want to take advantage of your options immediately. You'll save money on capital gains tax and income tax this way (see below). Also, if your exercise period is about to end, you should exercise your choices to lock in your lower pricing. However, if you're scared of losing money, you will have to get advice from an investing specialist.

### 1.9.3 Stocks Options and Taxes

You will almost always have to pay taxes when you activate or sell stock options. The price you pay will be determined by your choices and the time you wait for engaging and selling.

First of all, it's crucial to understand that there are two sorts of stock options:

The most popular are non-qualified stock options (NQSOs). The federal government does not provide corporations with any preferential tax benefit.

Executives with incentive stock options (ISOs) are granted preferential tax treatment.

The following table summarizes the significant tax variations among both NQSOs and ISOs:

If securities are transferred one year after the execution date and two years after the grant date, they are taxed as long-term capital gains. If sold before then, ordinary income taxes must be paid.

## Non-Qualified Stock Options (NQSOs) vs. Incentive Stock Options (ISOs)

| Tax Situation | NQSOs | ISOs |
|---|---|---|
| Exercise Date Taxes | Taxed as regular income. Must pay the difference between the stock's market value and the exercise price. | Do not have to pay taxes on the exercise date. Difference between the stock's market value and the exercise price could trigger the alternative minimum tax (AMT). |
| Sale Date Taxes | Must pay short-term capital gains on shares sold within one year of exercise date, and long-term capital gains on shares sold after at least one year. | |

# 1.10 How to Get Started in Options Trading

You may be wondering where to proceed since there are so many investment possibilities and many methods to trade them. However, after you've determined your objectives, getting started in options trading is simpler than you would think. Learn more about the fundamentals of options now, or contact us for more information on options trading.

### 1.10.1 Know What You Want

It's vital to have a clear notion of what you want to achieve before starting trading options. Options may play several roles in various portfolios, and deciding on a goal helps you cut down the field of possible methods. For instance, you can decide that you desire greater revenue from your assets. Perhaps you want to safeguard the value of your portfolio in the event of a market slump. No one aim is superior to another, and no alternative method is superior to another - it all depends on your objectives.

### 1.10.2 How to Get It

Once you've settled on a goal, you can start looking at other possibilities techniques to see if there's one or more that can help you achieve it. If you want to get extra money from your stocks, you may look at tactics like writing covered call options. If you want to safeguard your stocks from a market slump, you may consider buying puts, or options, on an index that follows the equities in your portfolio.

### 1.10.3 Are You Eligible

Your brokerage company will authorize you for a specified degree of options trading based on the information you submit in the options agreement. Because certain methods carry a high level of risk, not all investors are permitted to trade them. This regulation is intended to safeguard brokerage businesses against unskilled or underfunded investors who may fail on margin accounts. It has the potential to prevent investors from trading beyond their ability or financial resources. The number of stages of approval and needed credentials varies for each brokerage business, although it usually has four or five. The higher your approval level, the more trading experience you have and the more liquid assets you have to invest. Firms may also request that you acknowledge your understanding of the risks associated with options trading.

### 1.10.4 Getting the Paperwork Done

Even if you already have an investing account, there are still more procedures to do before you begin trading options. To begin, fill out an options agreement form, which is a document used by brokerage companies to assess your understanding of options and trading methods, as well as your overall investment expertise. Before you start trading options, read the Characteristics and Risks of Standardized Options paper, which offers essential information on options as well as comprehensive examples of the risks associated with certain contracts and techniques. Your brokerage company must disseminate it to all prospective option investors.

You may be unsure where to commence since there are many investment possibilities and methods to trade them. However, after you've determined your objectives, getting started in options trading is simpler than you would think. Learn more about the fundamentals of options now, or contact us for more information on options trading.

### 1.10.5 You Should Know What You Want

It's imperative to have a solid knowledge of what you want to achieve before starting trading options. Options may play several roles in various portfolios, and deciding on a goal helps you cut down the field of possible methods. For instance, you can decide that you desire greater revenue from your assets. Perhaps you want to safeguard the value of your portfolio in the event of a market slump. No one aim is superior to another, and no alternative method is superior to another - it all depends on your objectives.

### 1.10.6 Taking Care of the Paperwork

Even if you already have an investing account, there are still more procedures to do before you begin trading options. To begin, fill out an options agreement form, which is a document used by brokerage companies to assess your understanding of options and trading methods, as well as your overall investment expertise. Before you start trading options, read the Characteristics and Risks of Standardized Options paper, which offers essential information on options as well as comprehensive examples of the risks associated with certain contracts and techniques. Your brokerage company must disseminate it to all prospective option investors.

### 1.10.7 Keep an Eye on the Margins

Unlike stocks, you can't buy options on margin. Numerous options transactions, such as writing uncovered calls, are required by certain brokerage houses to be undertaken on a margin account. That implies if you write a call, you'll need to retain enough money in your account to pay the cost of buying the underlying equities if you execute the option. For uncovered writers, the margin requirement is set at a minimum of 20% of the underlying security minus the out-of-the-money option, but never less than 10% of the security value.

Your brokerage company will make a margin call or alert you that you need to contribute money to fulfill the minimum criteria if the value of the assets in your margin account falls below the needed maintenance level. Your brokerage business may liquidate assets in your investment account without authorization if you do not take the necessary measures. Because the value of options may fluctuate rapidly, it's critical to keep an eye on your options trading account to avoid being caught off guard by a margin call.

CHAPTER 2
# BASIC TERMS OF OPTIONS TRADING

Y ou'll notice that options traders utilize phrases exclusive to the options markets as you learn more about trading options. Understanding the meaning of terminology like strike price, exercise price, and expiry date are essential for successful options trading. You'll come across these words often, and comprehending them has a big impact on your chances of making money on an options transaction.

- **Strike Price**

The strike price of a call or put option is amongst the most significant trading concepts to understand. The striking price of a call option is the value at which a trader may purchase the contract's underlying assets. The striking valuation of a put option is the price at which the underlying stock may be sold. Whether a purchaser is "in the money" or "out of the money" is determined by the difference between one strike price at the time price of a stock.

- **Expiration Date**

Buying an options contract, unlike buying stock, is usually a shorter-term investment. When you purchase or sell an options contract, investors should indeed negotiate on a contract expiry date. You may pick the expiry cycle you want to invest in as a buyer or seller of an option. Usually quarterly, monthly, and weekly cycles for most stock options.

- **Time Decay**

In options trading, time decay is referred to as Theta. Theta denotes the change in the value of an option over tenure. Options will depreciate over time since they have an expiry date. Theta is the proportion from which an option's price depreciates over time. When purchasing options, it is essential to quit the transaction as soon as possible to avoid the effects of time decay eating into your earnings.

On the other hand, Theta works to the option seller's advantage since it is in the seller's best interests for the option to expire worthlessly. In addition, the rate at which the option price depreciates over time is not linear. Weekly options decay faster than monthly options, assuming all else remains constant.

- **In the money**

When contemplating stock fluctuations, it's common to think about whether a stock's price rises, falls, or stays the same. However, different terminology is utilized to indicate whether or not a transaction is repaying off when it comes to options. When the link between the strike price and the stock price supports the buyer, the option is in the money. Even having a call or a put option determines which direction this movement should go. A purchaser of a call option is in the finances if the strike price is lower than the stock's current price. Let's say you buy a call option to buy a stock at $50 per share, but the stock's actual price is $60 per share. You'd be up to $10 per share or in the black. Put options are the polar opposite of call options. If the strike price of either a put option is greater than the current stock price, the option buyer is in the money.

- **At the Money**

Another circumstance that the buyer of an option could face while trading options is being "at the money." The special and stock spot prices are the same in an at-the-money transaction. If the option buyer trades the option, people either profit or lose money. They will lose money if people implement the option due to the sheer deposit they paid.

- **Out the money**

Whenever a call or put option is out of the money, the option buyer will not profit financially by executing the option. The link between strike value and the price of stock influences how well a call or put option is in the money. When the strike price of a call option is higher than the current stock price, the option is out of money. When the strike price of a put option is less than the current stock price, the option is out of money.

- **Call Option**

Call Option is an option contract that provides the buyer (or holder) the right to buy and the seller (or writer) the duty to sell a certain number of shares (usually 100) of the underlying security at a set strike price on or before the contract's expiry date.

- **Put Option**

The buyer (or holder) has the right to sell, and the seller (or writer) has the responsibility to purchase a defined number of shares (usually 100) of the company's shares at a predetermined strike price sometime before the contract's expiry date.

- **Writer**

An Option Writer is a method of selling an option but does not have any long positions, which is similar to shorting a stock or index. If an option buyer executes his rights, the option writer earns a premium and is obligated to retain the agreement. When opposed to an option buyer, the option writer has a better chance of generating money. Market movement is a secondary element for option writers who speculate on time decay and volatility.

- **Holder**

The options holder is the participant that buys an option as the first (opening) transaction in options trading. An options trader uses a buy-to-open transaction to acquire an option. The options dealer is deemed long after purchasing it and can exercise it before the expiry date. The options holder will have to execute a sell-to-close deal to withdraw the long position.

- **Bid Price**

An investor's bid price is the amount they are inclined to purchase for securities.

For example, if a trader offered to sell a stock, they would have to establish how much someone would be ready to pay. This may be accomplished by examining the bid price. It shows the highest price for the stock that someone is prepared to pay.

- **Ask Price**

The ask price was set under which an investor may acquire an investment.

For example, if an investor wants to acquire stock, they must first figure out what someone is interested in selling it. They examine the asking price, the lowest price at which someone is prepared to sell a stock.

- **Insider Trading**

Insider trading is when someone else with non-public, substantial knowledge about a public company's shares trades in that stock for whatever purpose. Regardless of before the insider executes the deal, insider trading may be either unlawful or legal. When appropriate data is still categorized as privileged, insider trading is prohibited, and this kind of insider trading carries severe penalties.

- **Leverage**

You may control a bigger number of shares with a lesser quantity of money. Compared to owning a shorter or longer investment strategy, leverage offers options buyers with a higher profit potential while utilizing fewer funds. As a result, a 10% change in stock may be leveraged into something like a 100% or more gain by employing an option.

- **Wasting Assets**

A wasted asset is anything that has a finite lifespan and loses value irrevocably over time. Fixed assets, such as automobiles and equipment, depreciate over time, as do instruments with time decay, including options, which lose value after acquisition.

- **Leaps**

Long-term Equity Anticipation Securities (LEAPS) is an abbreviation for the phrase. LEAPS comprise put or call options whose expiry dates may be as far forward as 39 months in the future, depending on the market. Each LEAPS contract, like normal options, characterizes 100 shares of the stock market, similar to standard options.

- **Open Interest**

Open interest is the amount of options contracts that are now outstanding on a certain series of options contracts for a specific underlying stock.

- **Open Interest Configuration**

Open Interest Configuration (also known as open interest configuration) is the total wide variety of different contracts (also known as open interest) whatsoever strikes for a certain underlying security.

- **Opening price:**

The premium of a stock or option when purchased or sold for the first time on a certain day.

- **Opening Purchase**

An opening purchase (also known as a buy to open transaction) is when an investor becomes the owner of an option. This transaction enhances the value of the investor's long position while also increasing the amount of open interest in the option.

- **American Style**

In the financial world, an American option may be described as a sort of financial instrument that can be redeemed at any point in time between both the date of options trading and the expiry or maturity date of the option. American alternatives indeed tend to provide better flexibility, and this is one of the aspects why the latter is so generally popular and in high demand.

- **European Style**

A European option may be characterized as a call option that will only be redeemed at the option's expiry or maturity date rather than at any other time. Attributed to the fact that it has only one chance for exercise, European options are often marketed at a discount to their intrinsic value. European options are mostly traded over the counter, and they are less likely to be available on the major stock exchanges than other types of options.

- **Assignment**

When an option seller (writer) receives an exercise notice, they are obligated to sell (in the situation of a call) or acquire (in the context of a put) the preferred shares at the stated striking price.

- **Option Premium**

An option premium is a difference between the average current price of an option contract and the option contract's strike price. The money obtained by the seller (writer) from the sale of an option contract to a third party is referred to as the premium.

- **Intrinsic Value**

There is a variance in price between the strike and market prices of the financial commodity. Options in the money have inherent value, but options out of the money do not have this property.

- **Extrinsic Value**

Extrinsic value is measured as the change between the market rate of an option, also known as the premium, and its inherent value (also known as the strike price). Extrinsic value is sometimes referred to as the part of an option's valuation awarded to it by circumstances other than the underlying asset's price. On the other hand, the internal value is the intrinsic worth of choice, which is the inverse of extrinsic value.

- **Commission**

The commission is one of the expenses of doing business in the financial markets. The cost charged to a forex broker when joining or quitting a position is known as the transaction fee. Because commissions vary greatly, we recommend looking for companies that charge affordable prices.

- **Confirmation Statement**

After such an option strategy has been established or ended, a confirmation statement is given to the client by the brokerage business on behalf of the customer. The number of contracts purchased or sold and the amounts at which the exchanges took place are included in the statement. It's common for it to be used with a buy and selling statement.

- **Consensus Estimate**

When a firm publishes dividends quarterly, the experts who analyze that stock will use their profitability expectation for the company's quarterly performance, known as the consensus estimate. The consensus estimate is calculated by taking the average of all of these estimates. It is considered a good earnings surprise when actual results meet the analyst's expectations. Earnings that are lower than expected are referred to as negative surprises in earnings. Following these results disclosures, the stock market's response usually validates whether or not forecasts were high or low going into the financial results.

# CHAPTER 3

# GETTING STARTED WITH OPTIONS TRADING

Trades are made on one of the several regulated exchanges. Most options are available on many exchanges. Due to the standardized nature of option contracts, they may be traded across conversations. The following are the eleven extant option exchanges:

BOX Options Exchange
NASDAQ OMX PHLX
NYSE Arca Options
C2 Options Exchange
NYSE Amex Options
Chicago Board Options Exchange (CBOE)
BATS Options Exchange
NASDAQ Options Market
NASDAQ OMX BX
International Securities Exchange (ISE)
MIAX Options Exchange

The Options Clearing Corporation (OCC) is a financial services firm (OCC). The OCC was established in 1973 to operate as a clearinghouse for option contracts. It is the issuer and guarantee for options and futures contracts. The OCC should reassure investors that they will settle transactions, get premiums, and complete all assignments following the rules. The Securities and Exchange Commission has authority over it (SEC).

# 3.1 To Open a Trading Account

Before starting trading options, you'll need to create a brokerage account. There are various brokerage firms to choose from, including full-service and cheap brokers. The kind you select is determined by the quantity of guidance you need. Discount businesses provide lower costs but no personalized guidance. All major businesses provide various online information and calculators to help you with your financial selections.

- Charles Schwab
- Fidelity Investments
- Options press
- Interactive Brokers
- Trade Station
- trade Monster
- TD Ameritrade
- Merrill Edge
- Options House
- E*TRADE
- Place trade

After you've decided on a brokerage business, you'll choose between a cash account and a margin account. To borrow money to finance transactions, you'd utilize the collateral in a margin account. You may swap your account with the cash accessible in a cash account. If you pick a margin account, you'll be required to make a minimum deposit of $2,000 to create the account. A cash account usually needs no deposit or a minor payment to open it.

The quantity of cash and assets you must have differed per Brokerage Company in a margin account. If the sum falls below the necessary amount, the corporation will issue a margin call. It means you'll have to put more money into the account to meet their minimal criteria. The brokerage business will liquidate your assets if you don't do this. For this reason, you must be aware of your margin needs.

### 3.1.1 Agreement on Options

If you've already created an account, the next step is to execute an options agreement before you start trading options. This agreement explains your fundamental knowledge of trading options, financial loss-dealing capacities, and risk tolerance. After you finish the agreement, the brokerage business will assign you to an option acceptance level.

### 3.1.2 Making a Purchase

When they first start trading options, most novices believe it's merely a question of deciding which options to purchase and when to sell them. But it isn't that simple. Four basic types of orders may be made when buying and selling options. These four categories are bought to open, buy to close, sell to open, and sell to close. After picking one of these order forms, you must decide whether to complete it with a limit order or a market order. You must also enable your broker to differentiate the time of your order.

### 3.1.3 Types of Orders

The numerous types of orders are listed below.

To open, you must first purchase. The buy-to-open order is the quickest and most common way to place an order for options. It is used to acquire an options contract to establish a new position.

Purchase to complete the transaction. It's utilized to conclude a transaction with an established short place. You would place a purchase to close order if you had momentarily sold a certain options contract and wished to exit (close) the position. For example, if the value of the options contracts you sold has dropped, you may use a buy to close order to lock in your gains from these contracts and return to the reduced price. On the other hand, if the value of your short-selling options has increased and you want to prevent further losses, you may place a purchase order to terminate the trade and buy back the contracts, avoiding any more losses. Know whether you've taken a short position, in which case you benefit when the option's price falls, and you lose money when the cost of the vote rises.

Please make a sale to Open. This order is used to initiate a position on an options contract with the goal of short-selling it. This kind of order may be used when selling a covered call.

Sell to close the deal. It is decided to utilize the sell to close order. It's just the sequence in which you sell contracts for which you already have options. For calls or entries, the order is utilized.

### 3.1.4 Types of Fill Orders

#### What Are They and How Do They Work

After deciding on the kind of order you want, you must decide how to finish it. The possibilities include business orders, cap orders, stop orders, and stop-limit orders.

Your transaction takes place at a no greater price (if you purchase) or cheaper (if you sell) than the price level you designate in a restricted order. It prevents you from paying more for contracts than you thought or selling for less than you intended.

A market order would fulfill the order at the current selling price. It carries considerable risk since options prices frequently fluctuate, which means you might wind up buying or selling contracts at a greater or lower price than you anticipated.

It will fill a stop order when the price reaches the stop price. A stop-limit order combines the features of a stop order with those of a limit order.

### 3.1.5 Timings of Orders

You'll also need to indicate the order length or timing when making your order. Timing orders include day orders, all or none, fill or kill, good until canceled, good until date, or immediate or cancel.

An order for the day must be completed or canceled at the start of the trading day.

Orders must be completed in full or none at all. For example, if you want to buy 30 option contracts at a certain price but the broker can only buy 25 at that price, your request will be rejected. It's worth noting that, unlike a day order, this one remains open and does not expire at the end of the trading day, though you may cancel it at any moment.

The fill or destroy order is similar to an all or none order since automatically it cancels if it is not filled immediately.

The GTC order, or good until canceled, does not cancel unless canceled. This order will be accessible until you cancel it or it is completed.

The Good Till Date Order, or GTD, will stay open until the given date, at which point it will be canceled.

With one exception, the fill or destroy order, the immediate or cancel the order is similar to the fill or destroy order. If an order is completed quickly with this ordering method, but the rest is not, the unfilled contracts are canceled.

## 3.2 What Options Chains tell you An Overview

Options chains give important information for investors who wish to trade. Real-time choice chains are available on most financial websites and brokers.

Here's a quick rundown on how to interpret a chain of options.

The underlying stock's name, ticker symbol, exchange list, current market price, and volume are all included at the top of the table.

The option chain's columns include strike, symbol, last, change, bid, ask, volume, and open interest.

The strike price is shown in the first column for each option.

The option's symbol appears in the second column. The chain shows information for both calls (C) and puts (P) for each strike price (P).

The bid is the current price for the option buyers are interested in purchasing. The request is the price at which the seller is willing to sell.

The figure represents the number of contracts for exchange options on that particular day.

The number of available outstanding contracts is shown in the open interest column.

# 3.3 Making Deals

Whether you wish to trade online or over the phone, the actual execution technique is simple and follows the same approach.

### 3.3.1 Setting up the trade

To place a trade, you'll need the following:

The alternative's emblem

The kind of option is either a put or a call option.

The kind of order that has to be filled: purchase to make, purchase to make, sale to make, sale to make, purchase to make, purchase to make, purchase to make, purchase to make, purchase to make, purchase

The price of the strike

The expiry date

The price you're prepared to pay: Limits on the market or orders:

Timing of orders: order of the day, delicate till full, and so on.

### 3.3.2 Order acknowledgment

Before placing your order, double-check all information and make sure everything is correct. After you've placed your purchase, you'll get order confirmation. The request has yet to be approved, and it may be awaiting completion.

### 3.3.3 Trade Execution

Depending on the nature of your trade, it might take a few minutes, hours, or even days to complete your transaction. Once the order is filled, you should get a notification telling you the execution price.

### 3.3.4 Be patient

All you have to do now is keep an eye on your positions and stick to your plan.

## 3.4 Learning the Lingo

Options have their language, which might be difficult to grasp if unfamiliar with them. If you do know the language, though, everything becomes clearer. Fortunately, learning this language is not too tough.

The following factors constitute an option: - the kind of option (put or call) - the underlying security

- The first striking price
- The date of expiry
- You have the choice of paying a lower price or paying a higher price.

Typical options transactions include: - Buying a call for a debit to your account - Buying a put for a debit to your account - Selling a call for a credit to your account - Selling a put for a credit to your account - Selling a call for a credit to your account - Selling a put for a credit to your account

Contracts are used for trading options, and each contract controls 100 shares of the underlying securities.

You sign into a contract to purchase a call from the call seller when you buy a call to start a fresh position. You engage into a contract to purchase a put from the put seller when you buy a put to start afresh put position.

You get into a contract to sell a call to the call buyer when you sell a call to open a fresh position. You get into a contract to sell the put to the put buyer when you sell to open a fresh position.

After you've opened an option position, you'll need to perform one of the following things before it expires:

- Close the contract by selling the long call or put position - Buy back the short call or put position - Exercise the long call or put option at the strike price

Allow the option to expire worthless if they run out of money before the deadline.

Finally, even though it's rare, you should be ready to take an assignment if you're short a call or a put. It is an area that many new option traders are concerned about, but it is unneeded. Assignments don't happen very frequently, but when they do, they're simple to deal with, as we'll see soon.

The option price, sometimes known as the premium, comes next. It is paid or earned as a premium for buying or selling options.

The premium is made up of two parts:

- Worth on its own
- Importance of extrinsic factors (time value)
- If the gap between the strike price and the current market price of the underlying asset is advantageous to the option buyer, intrinsic value is calculated.

The period till expiry determines the extrinsic value. The time value decreases as the time till expiry decreases.

Let's imagine you had a call option with a strike price of $40, and the stock was trading at $45. The difference between $45 and the strike price of $40 would represent the intrinsic value of that option, which would be $5. Let's imagine the option was set to expire in 90 days. It would have extrinsic or temporal value in addition to the $5 intrinsic worth. And depending on the implied volatility of the option, with 90 days till expiry, such an option would most likely have $2 of extrinsic value. So, at that moment in time, the overall worth of that choice may be $7, with $5 of intrinsic value and $2 of extrinsic or temporal value.

No matter what happens to the underlying asset, your risk as a buyer of a call or a put to establish a fresh position is now restricted to the purchase price. Theoretically, your earning potential is limitless.

Your risk as a seller of a call to initiate a fresh position is potentially infinite for a short call position. Why? Because the stock, or underlying asset, might soar to unimaginable heights, putting you in danger. The amount of money you can make is restricted by the amount of credit.

Now, your risk as a seller of a put to initiate a new position is the difference between the strike price and zero, minus the credit obtained for a short position. So, if you were short a $40 strike put option and earned a $1 credit for shorting it, and the price dropped to zero, you'd lose $40 minus the $1, or $39. In addition, the amount of money you may make is restricted by the amount of credit you have.

As you can see, implementing multiple choices techniques is crucial. And, once again, if you don't use them correctly, you'll find yourself in a dangerous scenario. However, if you do, options may help you reduce risk and are less dangerous than trading the underlying stock or ETF.

### Assignment

Assignment seldom occurs and even less often when weekly choices are available.

However, there is no need to be alarmed if this does occur. Allow no one to make you afraid of a task.

If the market is in-the-money relative to your short option, you may be assigned, which means the put or call holder may execute their option.

It will be done automatically by the broker, who will notify you that you have been allocated.

So, suppose you don't have any other strategies. In that case, you advise the broker or go to the broker's online trading platform to instantly purchase back the stock shares in the event of a call assignment or sell the stock shares in the case of a put assignment, and you're out of the trade.

That is all there is to it. That's all there is to it!

# 3.5 Pay of Diagrams

A pay-off or breakeven diagram depicts the strategy's potential profit or loss at various stock values upon expiration. Pay-off diagrams may be produced for every choice or combination of options in a single class.

Under "Prices and research," pick "Calculators," and utilize the strategy modeling tool in the options area of the ASX website, asx.com.au.

### 3.5.1 Taker of a call option

An example is buying a three-month Woolworths Ltd (WOW) $27.00 call for 50 cents.

## WOW $27.00 call option

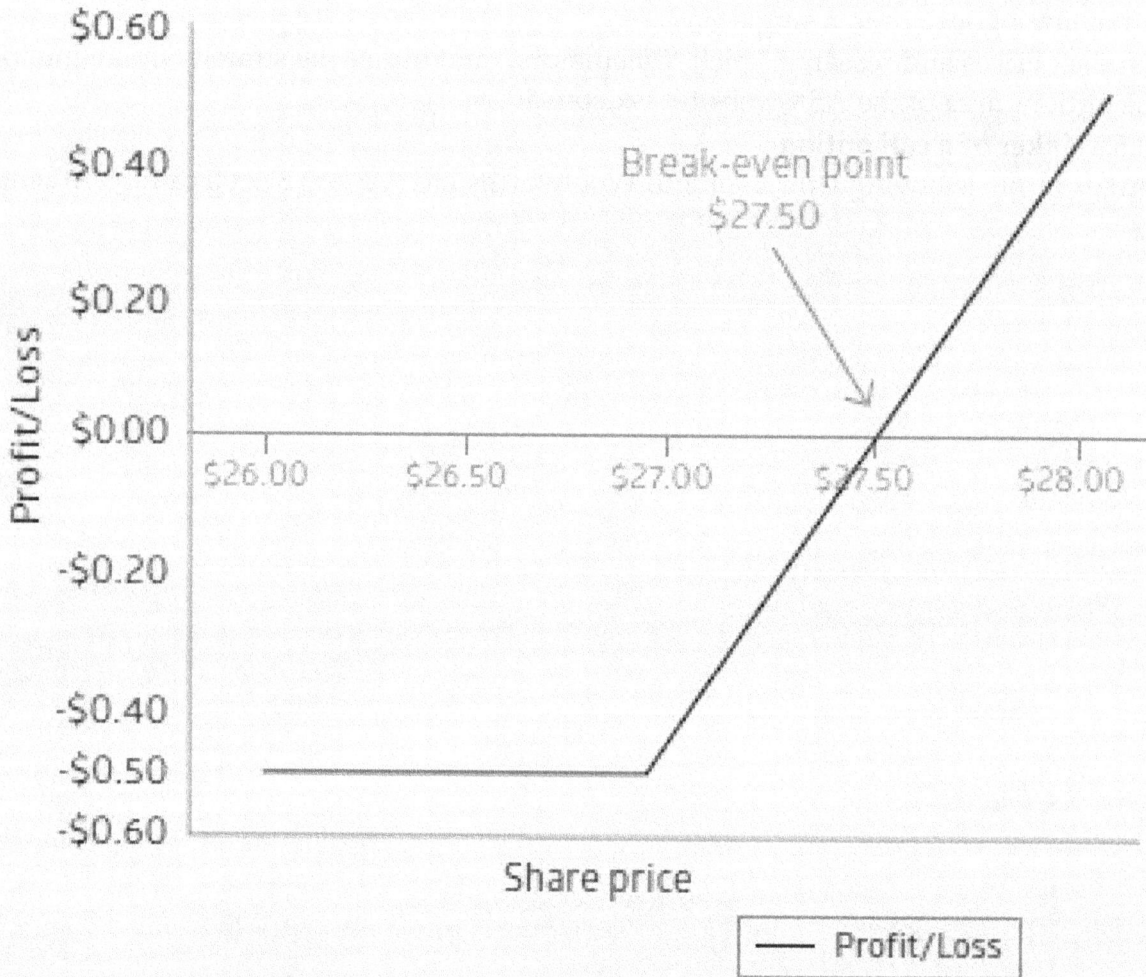

The option's exercise price plus the premium paid is the call option taker's breakeven point. It costs $27.50 ($27.00 workout fee + 50 cent extra) in this case.

The chart illustrates that the call option taker has an unrealized loss when WOW is below $27.50. The premium paid by the call option taker is the maximum the call option taker may lose (50 cents). The call option taker starts to benefit when the WOW share price goes over $27.50.

The maximum profit is infinite since the taker's profit is higher the share price climbs.

### 3.5.2 Writer of call options

Let's say you're selling a $29.00 ANZ call for $1.00.

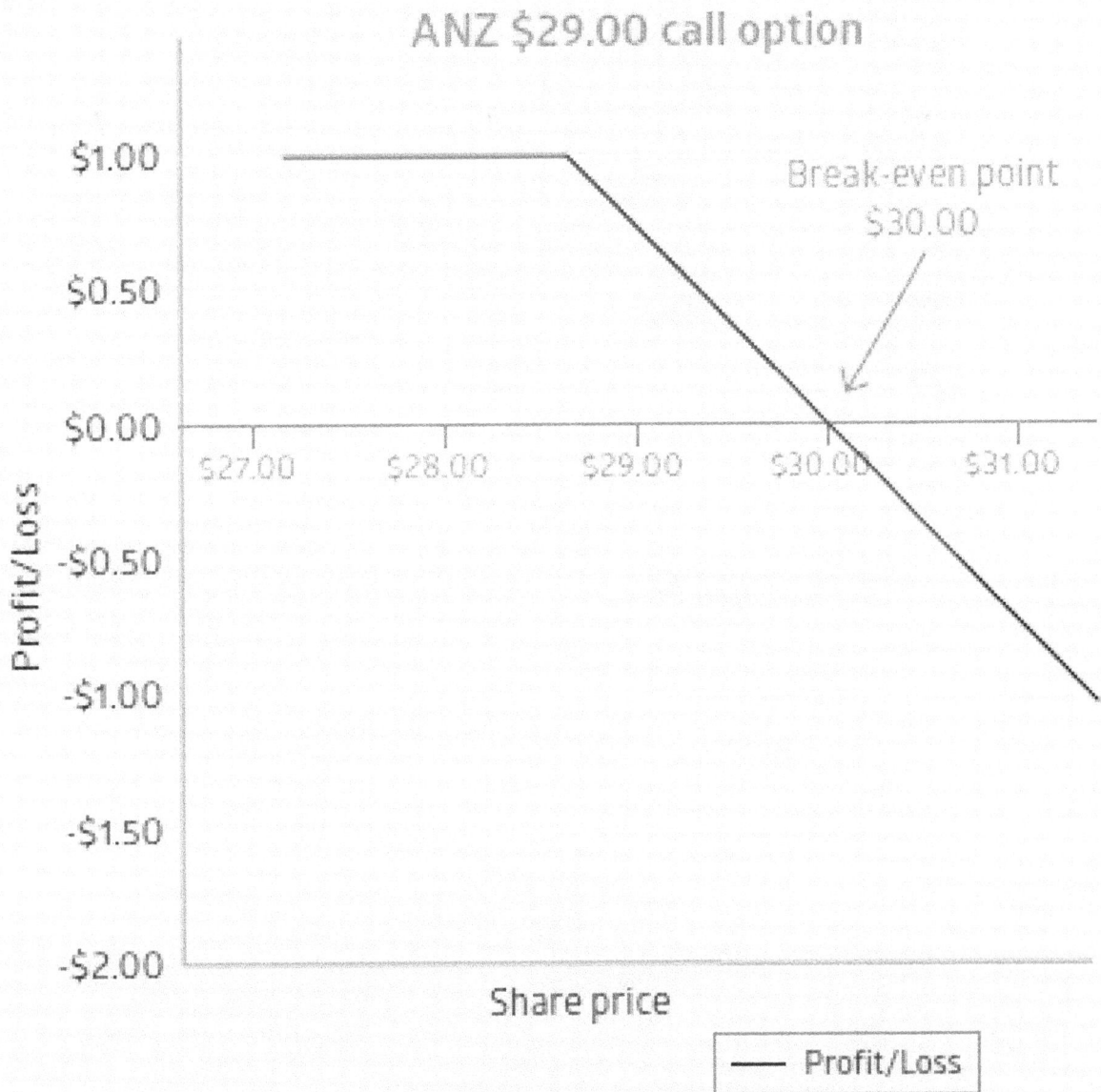

ANZ $29.00 call option

Break-even point
$30.00

Profit/Loss

Share price

—— Profit/Loss

Profit is restricted to the premium ($100) obtained. The potential loss is limitless if the option writer does not hold the underlying shares. If the option is exercised, the writer will have to pay more to acquire the shares at the market price as the share price increases. The call option writer's breakeven point equals the option's exercise price plus the premium received. It is the same as the taker of a call option.

### 3.5.3 Taker of put options

An example is buying a three-month BlueScope Steel Ltd (BSL) $14.00 put for 20 cents.

## BSL $14.00 put option

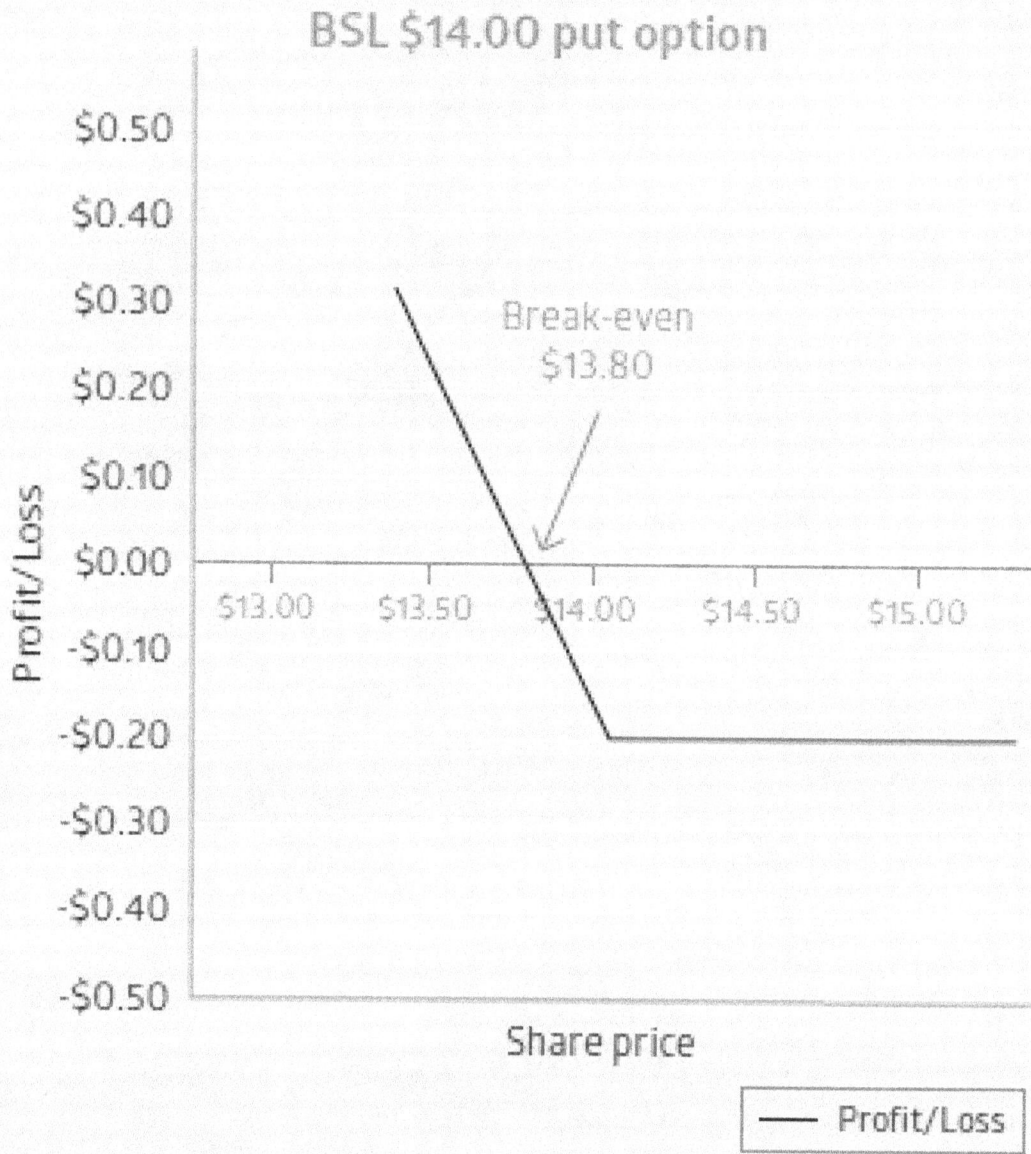

The diagram shows that the put option taker can only lose the premium paid. The greater the investor's potential profit, the lower the share price below the breakeven threshold of $13.80. The exercise price minus the premium paid is the put option taker's breakeven point. The exercise price less the premium paid equals the maximum profit.

### 3.5.4 Writer as an option

Selling a one-month CPU $16.50 put for ten cents is an example.

## CPU $16.50 put option

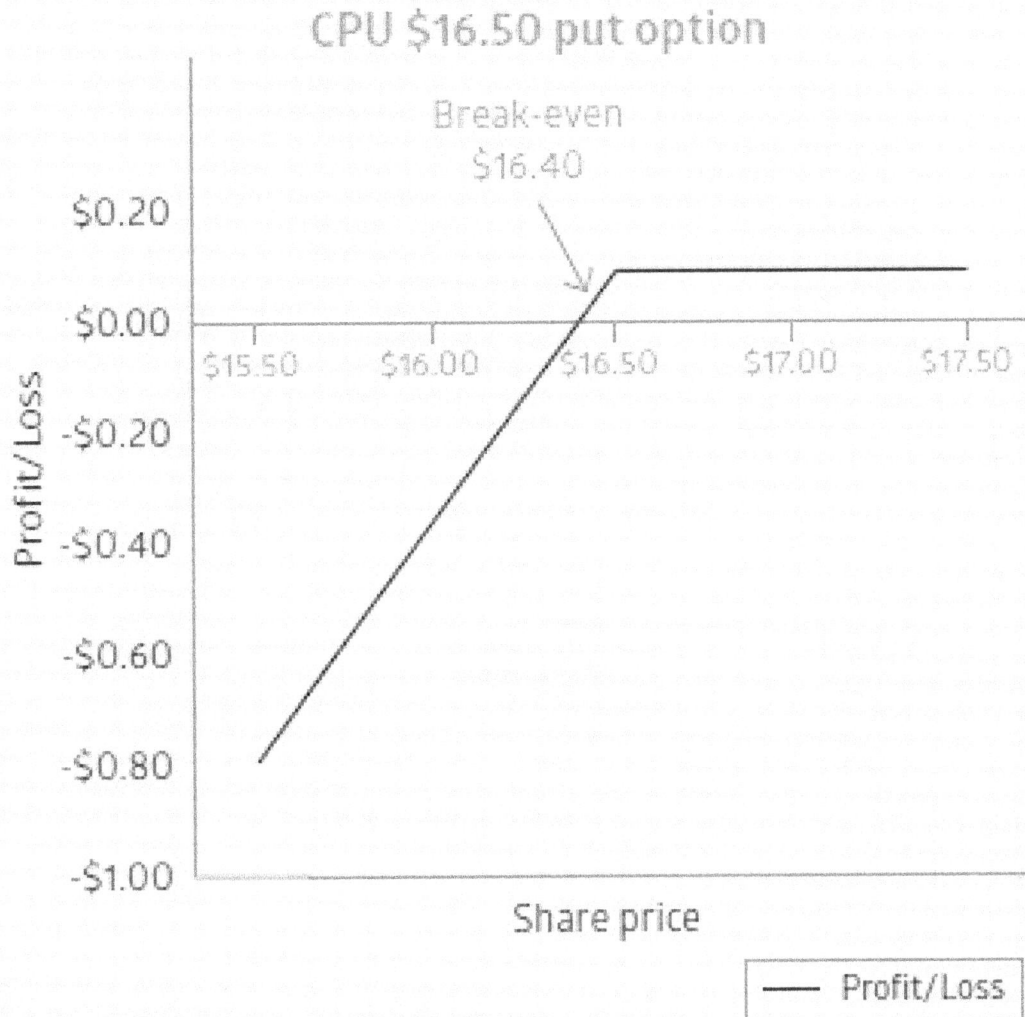

The put option writer's profit potential is restricted to the premium received ($10), as shown in the diagram. Put writers' earnings decrease whenever the stock price goes below $16.50. After the stock price goes below $16.40, this becomes a loss. The exercise price minus the premium paid equals $16.40, and the potential loss is limited only by a drop in the share price to $0.

| CALL OPTION TAKER | CALL OPTION WRITER |
|---|---|
| **Characteristics** | **Characteristics** |
| Pays premium | Receives premium |
| Right to exercise and buy the shares | Obligation to sell shares if exercised |
| Benefits from rising volatility | Benefits from time decay |
| Profits from price rising | Profits from price falling or remaining neutral |
| Limited losses, potentially unlimited gain | Potentially unlimited losses, limited gain |
| Can sell before expiry to close out | Can buy back before expiry or before assignment to close out |

| PUT OPTION TAKER | PUT OPTION WRITER |
|---|---|
| **Characteristics** | **Characteristics** |
| Pays premium | Receives premium |
| Right to exercise and sell shares | Obligation to buy shares if exercised |
| Benefits from rising volatility | Benefits from time decay |
| Profits from price falling | Profits from price rising or remaining neutral |
| Limited losses, gain is only limited to the share price falling to zero | Losses only limited to the share price falling to zero, limited gain |
| Can sell before expiry to close out | Can buy back before expiry or before assignment to close out |

# 3.6 Fundamentals of Technical Analysis for Options Trading

### 3.6.1 What is the definition of technical analysis

Technical analysis is a technique for predicting an asset's likely future price movement based on market data, such as a stock or currency pair.

The validity of technical analysis is based on the idea that all market participants' aggregate activities - buying and selling – properly reflect all relevant information about a traded asset and, as a result, continuously assign a fair market value to the security.

It's essentially chart reading. It is the science (or art) of spotting chart patterns, interpreting them to make buying and selling timing choices, and putting a trading strategy into action. Technical analysis may help you not only make better judgments but also make them more precisely, more disciplined, and more successfully manage your money.

Many followers of the technical analysis think that glancing at the charts will reveal all you need to know about an investment.

There are two types of technical analysis:

- Price patterns are simply visual patterns of what is going on with the security's price.
- Indicators are mathematical algorithms that take all components of price movement, including volume, and combine them to generate various ratios and analyses that may be used to forecast future price movement.

### 3.6.2 Price History as a Predictor of Future Results

Technical traders think that the market's current or previous price activity is the most accurate predictor of future price action.

Technical analysis is employed by more than only technical traders. Many fundamental traders utilize fundamental analysis to decide whether to buy into a market, then employ technical analysis to find appropriate, low-risk buy entry price levels after they've made that choice.

### 3.6.3 Different Time Frames for Charting

Technical traders analyze price charts to forecast price movement. The evaluation time frames and technical indicators that a trader decides to use are the two most important elements in technical analysis.

Technical analysis time frames on charts may vary from one minute to monthly or even annual. The following are some of the most common periods that technical analysts look at:

- Chart for 5 minutes
- Chart for 15 minutes
- Hourly graph
- 4-hour graph

- Daily Chart

The time range that a trader studies is usually defined by their particular trading strategy. Intra-day traders like to analyze price movement on shorter time frame charts, such as the 5-minute or 15-minute charts, since they initiate and terminate trading positions inside a single trading day. Long-term traders who maintain market positions overnight or for extended periods are more likely to use hourly, 4-hour, daily, or even weekly charts to assess markets.

For an intra-day trader seeking a chance to benefit from price swings that occur throughout one trading day, price movement that happens inside a 15-minute time window may be quite important. However, the same price movement may not be as noteworthy or predictive for long-term trading objectives on a daily or weekly chart.

Viewing the same price movement on several time frame charts is easy to demonstrate this. The following daily chart for silver shows the price trading in the same range as it has for many months, about $16 to $18.50. Because the price is so close to the low end of that range, a long-term silver investor could be tempted to purchase silver.

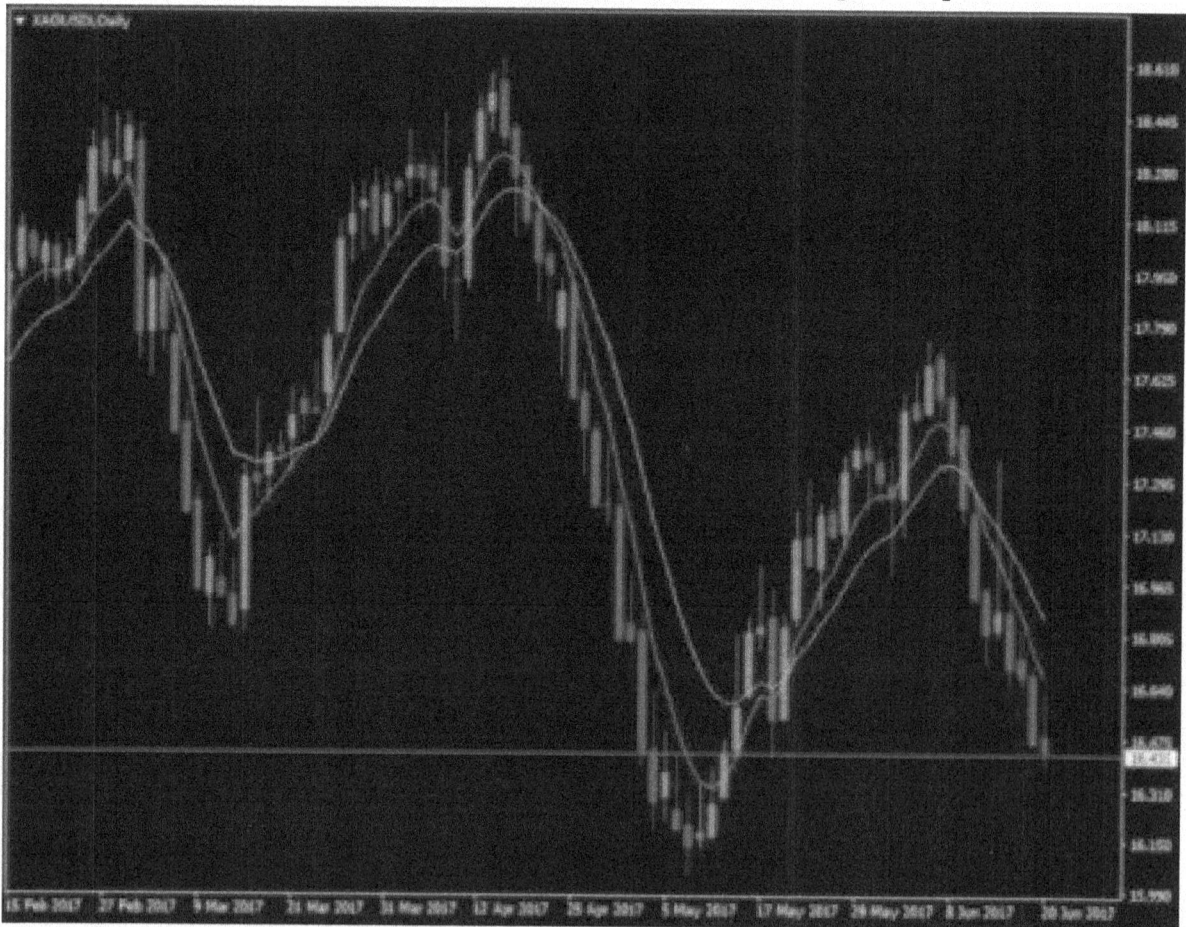

However, an hourly chart of the same price action (below) reveals a continuous drop that has increased somewhat in the last several hours. Based on the hourly chart price movement, a silver trader interested in making intra-day trades would probably avoid purchasing the precious metal.

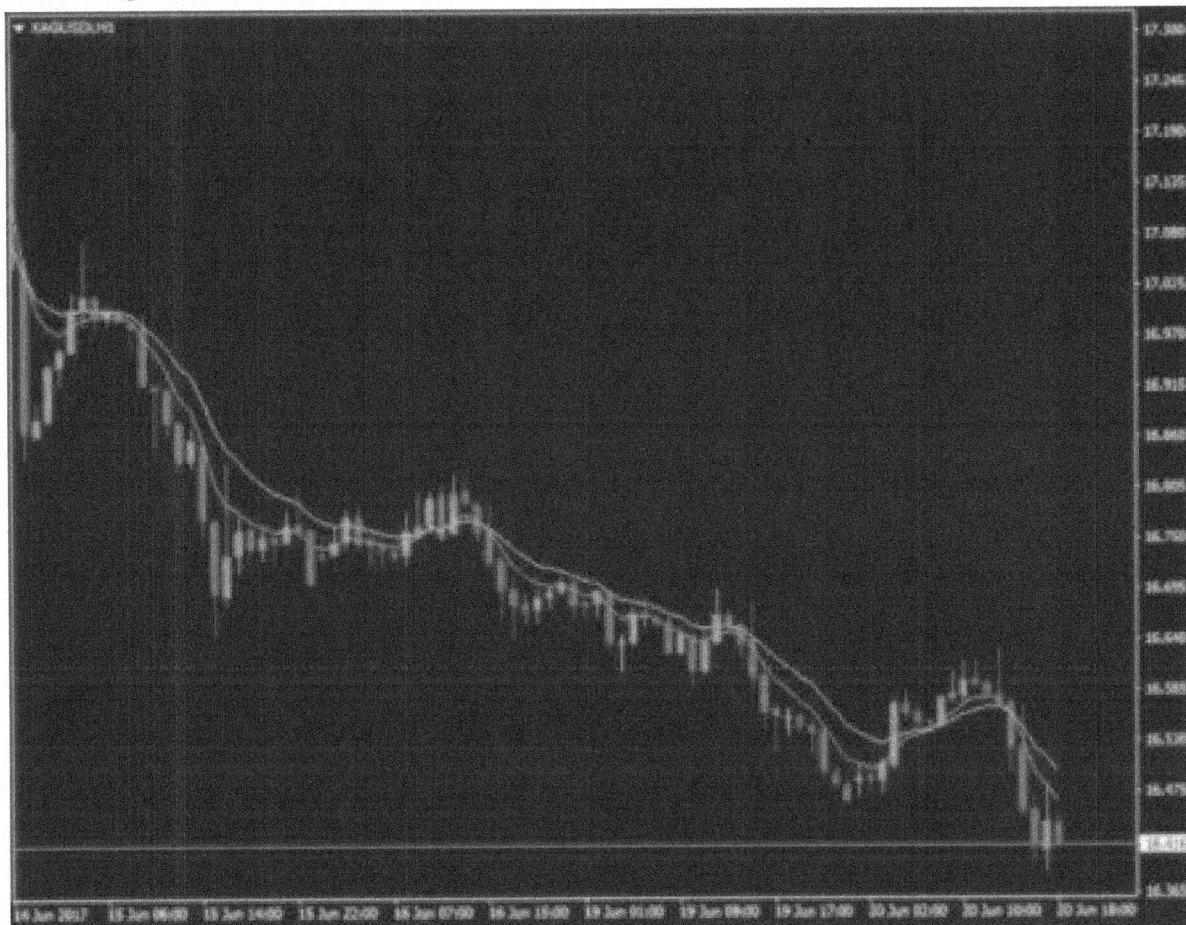

### 3.6.4 Three Ways to Look at Price Trends

Simply said, price patterns are the patterns of a security's price changes over time. Price activity may be seen in three ways for any length of time:

- Simple line graphs
- Bar graphs
- Japanese candlesticks

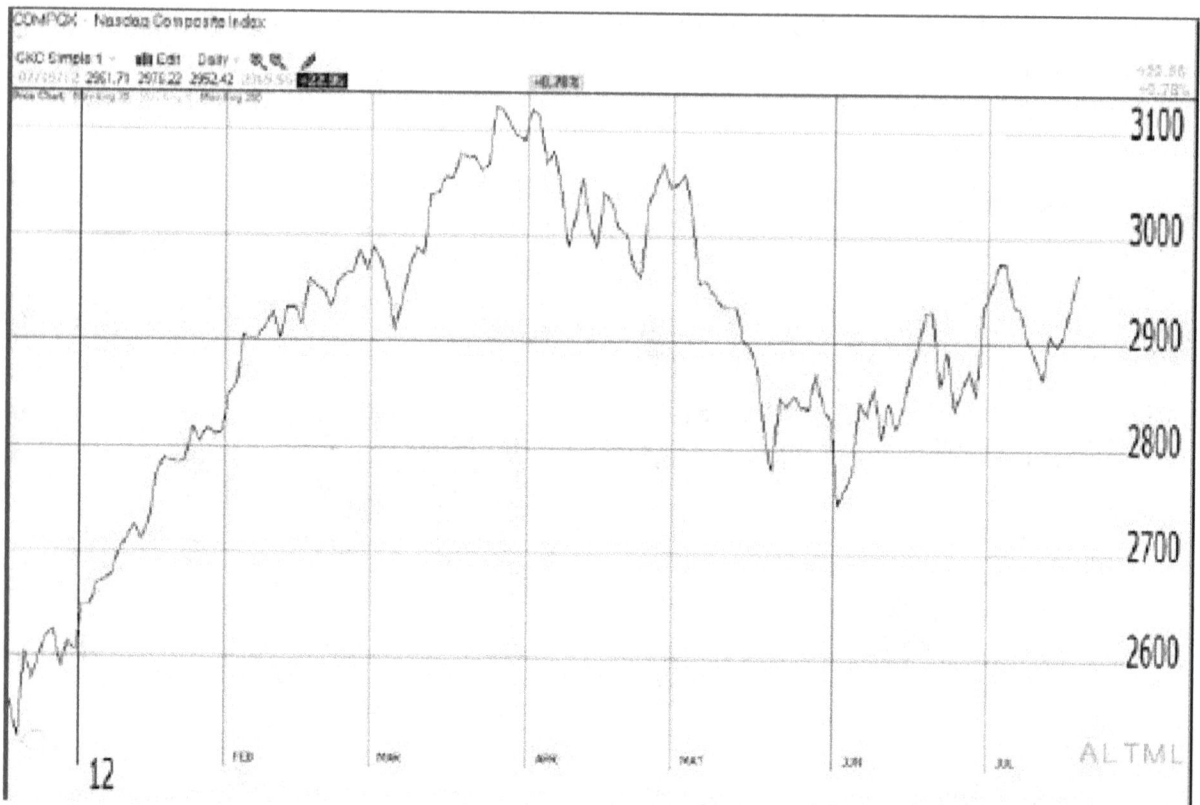

Simple NASDAQ daily line chart from December 2011 to July 2012.

Although you can see that the price has varied from just under 2600 in December 2011 to over 3100 in March 2012, this chart is rather worthless in and of itself.

Simple line graphs show the line crossing at the mean of the high and low for each time (in this case, the line crosses at the mean of the high and low for each day, since this is a daily chart).

A more helpful chart would be one that depicted daily prices in such a manner that the high, low, open, and close for each day could be seen.

This chart shows a Simple NASDAQ daily open bar chart from December 2011 to July 2012.

Keep in mind that each period (in this case, a day) is represented by a vertical bar. Also, observe how each bar has a tiny horizontal line to the left and a little horizontal line to the right. These lines represent the NASDAQ's opening and closing prices for each day. The high and low prices obtained on that specific day are represented by the tops and bottoms of each vertical line.

# 3.7 Candlesticks

The most frequent way of displaying price movement on a chart is candlestick charting. The price activity produces a candlestick over a specific time for every time frame. On an hourly chart, each candlestick represents the price movement for one hour, while on a 4-hour chart, each candlestick represents the price action for every 4 hours.

The following is how candlesticks are "drawn" / formed: The highest point on a candlestick represents the highest price securities traded during that period, while the lowest point represents the lowest price. The opening and closing prices for the time are shown by the "body" of a candlestick (the corresponding red or blue "blocks," or thicker sections, of each candlestick as seen in the charts above). A blue candlestick body means the closing price (top of the candlestick body) was higher than the opening price (bottom of the candlestick body); a red candlestick body means the opening price was higher than the closing price.

Colors for candlesticks are chosen at random. Some traders employ white and black candlestick bodies (the usual color format and hence the most prevalent); others use green and red, blue and yellow, or other combinations. Whatever colors are used, they make it simple to see if a price closed higher or lower after a certain period at a glance. The analyst obtains more visual clues and patterns when using candlestick charts for technical analysis than a basic bar chart.

### 3.7.1 Doji Candlestick Patterns

Candlestick patterns, which may be made up of a single candlestick or a series of two or three, are among the most extensively used technical indicators for detecting future market reversals or trend changes.

Doji candlesticks, for example, reflect market hesitation and might foreshadow an upcoming trend shift or market reversal. A Doji candlestick is distinguished because the beginning and closing prices are the same, resulting in a flat candlestick body. The greater the hint of market uncertainty and possible reversal, the longer the upper and lower "shadows," or "tails," on a Doji candlestick — the candlestick component representing the low-to-high range for the period.

Doji candlesticks come in various shapes and sizes, each with its name, as illustrated in the figure below.

**Long-legged Indecision**    **Dragonfly** Bullish    **Gravestone** Bearish    **Four Price**

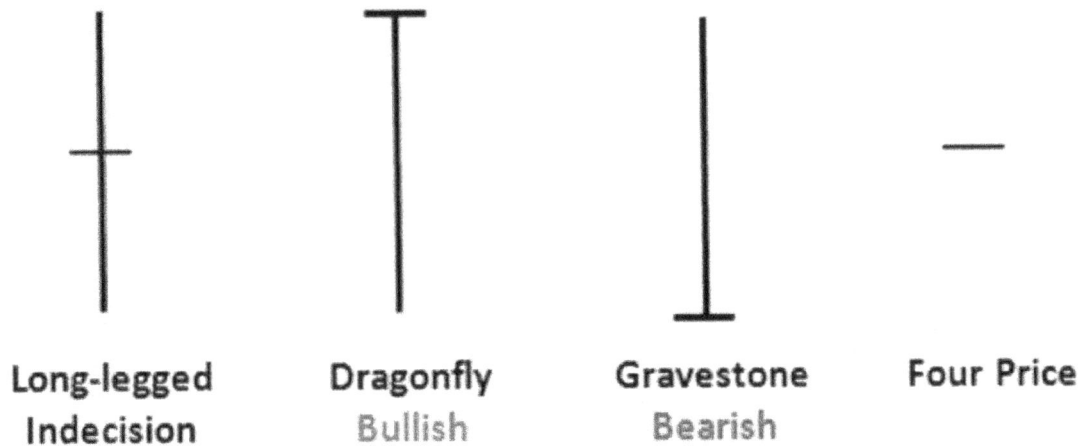

The long-legged doji is a kind of Doji in which the price range is almost equal in both directions and opens and closes in the center of the price range for the period. The emergence of the candlestick conveys market hesitation in a clear visual manner. When a Doji develops after a market has been in a lengthy uptrend or downturn, it is generally viewed as indicating a likely market reversal or a trend shift in the opposite direction.

The dragonfly doji appears after a protracted decline indicates an impending positive reversal. The logical meaning of the dragonfly doji is explained by looking at the price activity suggested by it. The dragonfly indicates sellers driving price down (the long lower tail), but the price rebounds to close at its greatest position after the cycle. The candlestick suggests that the prolonged push to the downside has been rejected.

The name of the tombstone Doji implies that it symbolizes terrible news for purchasers. The tombstone Doji, which is the polar opposite of the dragonfly formation, signals a strong rejection of an effort to drive market prices upward, indicating a likely reverse reversal

The four-price Doji, which occurs when the market opens, closes, and conducts all buying and selling at the same price during the period, is the embodiment of indecision. This market has no desire to move anyplace in particular.

There are hundreds of candlestick forms to choose from and various pattern variants. Thomas Bulkowski's pattern site is perhaps the most comprehensive resource for detecting and using candlestick patterns. It extensively describes each candlestick pattern and even offers data on how frequently each pattern has historically provided a good trading signal. Knowing what a candlestick pattern means is useful, but whether that indicator has shown to be correct 80 percent of the time is much more so.

### 3.7.2 Moving Averages are a kind of technical indicator

Technical traders may use an almost limitless number of technical indicators to help them make trading choices in addition to analyzing candlestick patterns.

Moving averages are perhaps the most popular technical indicator. One or more moving averages are used in many trading methods. "Buy as long as price continues above the 50-period exponential moving average (EMA); sell as long as price remains below the 50 EMA," for example, is a basic moving average trading strategy.

Another often-used technical indication is moving average crossovers. When the 10-period moving average crosses over the 50-period moving average, a crossover trading strategy may be to purchase.

The higher the moving average figure, the more important price change is deemed about it. Price passing above or below a 100- or 200-period moving average, for example, is often seen as much more important than price crossing above or below a 5-period moving average.

### 3.7.3 Pivots and Fibonacci Numbers are two technical indicators

Many traders use daily pivot point indicators to indicate price levels for entering and exiting trades. These indicators frequently identify many support and resistance levels in addition to the pivot point. Significant support or resistance levels and levels where trade is confined within a range are commonly marked by pivot point levels. Many traders interpret trading that soars (or plummets) through the daily pivot and all accompanying support or resistance levels as "breakout" trading, which will change market prices significantly higher or lower in the breakout direction.

The previous trading day's high, low, opening, and closing prices construct daily pivot points and their related support and resistance levels. I'd explain to you how to do it, but there's no need since pivot point levels are generally publicized every trading day, and there are pivot point indicators you can put on a chart that perform the math for you and disclose pivot levels. The daily pivot point is usually shown with three price support levels below it and three price resistance levels above it in most pivot point indicators.

### 3.7.4 Fibonacci Retracements

Another common technical analysis method is Fibonacci levels. Fibonacci was a 12th-century mathematician who created a set of ratios that technical traders often use. Fibonacci ratios, often known as levels, are widely utilized to identify trading opportunities and profit goals that develop during long-term trends.

0.24, 0.38, 0.62, and 0.76 are the basic Fibonacci ratios. These are often stated as percentages - 23%, 38%, etc. It's worth noting that Fibonacci ratios work well together: 24 percent is the opposite, or remaining, of 76 percent, and 38 percent is the opposite, or remainder, of 62 percent.

Various free technical indicators will automatically compute and load Fibonacci levels into a chart, much like pivot point levels.

The most often used Fibonacci indicator is Fibonacci retracements. There is often a corrective retracement in the opposite direction after a security has been in a prolonged uptrend or downturn for some time before the price continues the general long-term trend. Fibonacci retracements are utilized to discover appropriate, low-risk trading entry locations during a retracement.

Assume that stock "A" has constantly increased from $10 to $40. The stock price then starts to decline somewhat. Many investors would hunt for a favorable entry-level to purchase shares during a price pullback.

According to Fibonacci statistics, price retracements are anticipated to be 24 percent, 38 percent, 62 percent, or 76 percent of the upward rise from $10 to $40. Investors are looking for signs that the market is finding support at these levels, from which price will begin to rise again. For example, if you were looking for an opportunity to purchase the stock following a 38 percent price retracement, you may place a buy order around the $31 price level. (Moving from $10 to $40 equals $30; 38% of $30 equals $9; $40 – $9 = $31)

### 3.7.5 Extensions of the Fibonacci Sequence

Continuing with the previous scenario, you've purchased the stock for $31 and are attempting to calculate a profit objective at which to sell it. Fibonacci extensions may help with this since they show how much a higher price can go when the broader uptrend continues. The Fibonacci extension levels are derived from the bottom of the retracement and represent 126 percent, 138 percent, 162 percent, and 176 percent of the initial uptrend move. So, suppose the retracement low is a 38 percent retracement of the initial move from $10 to $40. In that case, you may determine the first Fibonacci extension level and probable "take profit" goal by adding 126 percent of the original $30 move higher to that price ($31). The following is the formula:

The 126 percent Fibonacci extension level is $31 + ($30 x 1.26) = $68 - giving you a target price of $68.

Again, you'll never have to do any of these computations. Simply insert a Fibonacci indicator into your charting program to see all Fibonacci levels.

Even if you don't utilize pivot and Fibonacci levels as indicators in your trading approach, they're worth following. Because so many traders base their buying and selling decisions on pivot and Fibonacci levels, there is likely to be a lot of trading activity around those price points, which may help you better predict future price movements.

### 3.7.6 Momentum Indicators - Technical Indicators

Like most other technical indicators, moving averages are designed to predict market direction, whether it's up or down.

However, there is another class of technical indicators whose primary aim is to identify market strength rather than market direction. The Stochastic Oscillator, the Relative Strength Index (RSI), the Moving Average Convergence-Divergence (MACD) indicator, and the Average Directional Movement Index are examples of these indicators (ADX).

Momentum indicators assist investors in deciding whether the current price movement is more likely to reflect relatively inconsequential, range-bound trade or a genuine, major trend by analyzing the strength of price movement. Because momentum indicators quantify trend strength, they may be used to predict when a trend is about to terminate. For example, if a security has been in a strong, long-term uptrend for many months, but one or more momentum indicators indicate that the trend is losing strength, it may be time to consider taking gains.

The USD/SGD 4-hour chart below demonstrates the importance of a momentum indicator. Below the main chart window, the MACD indicator displays in a secondary window. The steep upturn in the MACD, which began around June 14th, suggests that the matching price increase is a strong, ongoing advance rather than a one-time corrective. The MACD displays weaker price action as the price starts to retrace lower on the 16th, suggesting that the downward movement in price does not have much momentum behind it. A robust rise continues shortly after that. In this case, the MACD would have reassured a market buyer that (A) the price increase to the upside was strong and (B) that the uptrend was likely to continue when the price dropped slightly on the 16th.

Because momentum indicators simply indicate strong or weak price movement rather than trend direction, they are often used in conjunction with other technical analysis indicators as part of a trading strategy.

### 3.7.7 Conclusion of the Technical Analysis

It's important to remember that no technical indication is flawless. None of them consistently provide signs that are 100 percent correct.

The most astute traders are constantly on the lookout for clues that the signals generated by their selected indicators may be false. Technical analysis, when done correctly, may significantly increase your trading profitability. Spending more time and effort thinking about managing things if the market swings against you, rather than daydreaming about how you're going to spend your millions, may do more to enhance your trading fortunes.

# 3.8 How to Calculate Probability

### 3.8.1 What does POP (PROBABILITY OF PROFIT) mean

The possibility of earning at least $0.01 on a deal is the Probability of profit (POP). This is an intriguing indicator that is influenced by various factors in trading, including whether we're buying or selling options or lowering the cost basis of stock, we're long or short.

### 3.8.2 When Selling Options, the Probability of Profit

We sell options at strikes that are at the money (where the stock price is trading) or out of the money (where the stock price is trading) (at a better price than where the stock price is trading). Knowing this, we may infer that if we feel that purchasing or selling shares outright would result in a coin flip opportunity, we will have a larger than 50% chance of succeeding. With techniques like these, we also have more opportunities to succeed. When selling an option, the stock price may remain the same, move in our favor, or move slightly against us and we'll still be profitable after expiry. The capacity to produce money in various methods increases the likelihood of overall success.

When we sell options, we get a credit, which is money. This credit may be utilized as a cushion against losses on our position, increasing our chances of succeeding even more. We can continually enhance our POP using premium-selling tactics since our breakeven price is directly tied to our POP, which is improved by selling premium.

### 3.8.3 When Buying Options, the Probability of Profit

When we say "purchase options," we typically mean "buy spreads." Buying a naked option is the worst thing we can do for our breakeven since we have no method of hedging the cost of the option. We cling to spreads because of this. When purchasing spreads, we aim to acquire a breakeven price that is extremely near to or slightly better than the current stock price. It guarantees a POP of approximately 50% or somewhat better.

### 3.8.4 Probability of Profit & Cost Reduction on a Cost Base

One of the best things about owning stock is adding a free short call to the transaction. That instantly puts money (not profit) in our pockets and does not need more purchasing power. We may collect premium by selling one call for every 100 shares of stock we possess and utilize it to lower the cost basis of our stock. It increases the likelihood of success in stock purchases from a 50/50 coin flip to a substantially greater probability of success. When we sell the call, the stock may now remain exactly where it is, go up or down a little bit, and we can still profit based on the credit we get. We never know where a stock will go, so we concentrate on increasing the one thing we can control: cost basis.

# 3.9 Top Indicator to Use

Binary options enable traders to place conditional bets on predetermined values of stock indices, currency, commodities, and events in a time-bound manner. Each binary option has an option premium ($45, $81, and $77 in the instances above), a predetermined strike price ($1,700, 8600 points, and 108 yen), and an expiration date, much like a conventional exchange-traded option (1:30 p.m., 2 p.m., 3 p.m. today).

The differentiator is the settlement price, which stays constant at $0 or $100 depending on whether the option condition is met. It maintains a constant net profit (or loss). The option premium is also set at a range of $0 to $100.

### 3.9.1 Probability Calculation

Probability calculations play an essential role in pricing binary options since they are time-bound and condition-based. "What is the possibility that the present gold price of $1,220 will go to $1,250 or higher in the next four hours?" it all comes down to. The following are the deciding factors:

- Volatility (how much, and is it enough to breach the strike price threshold?)
- The price movement's direction
- Timing

The criteria above should be included in technical indicators for binary options trading. A binary option position may be taken to detect sustained momentum or trend reversal patterns. Let's look at some of the most often used binary option technical indicators.

### 3.9.2 DMI of Wilder (ADX)

Wilder's Directional Movement Indicators (DMI) Average Directional Index (ADX) tries to reflect the strength of an already defined trend by combining three lines, namely ADX, DI+, and DI-, and their relative locations. The table below may be used to understand the trends.

| Position | Momentum | ADX Value > 25 | ADX Value < 25 |
|----------|----------|----------------|----------------|
| DI+ above DI- | Indicates Uptrend | Strong Uptrend | Weak, Unsustainable Uptrend |
| DI- above DI+ | Indicates Downtrend | Strong Downtrend | Weak, Unsustainable Downtrend |

A suitable buy/sell position might be made based on the detected momentum and trend strength.

### 3.9.3 The pivotal point

Pivot point analysis (in combination with support and resistance levels) aids in determining trends and directions over time. Pivot points may be employed for binary options because of their time flexibility, especially when trading highly liquid major currencies. Using Pivot Points in Forex Trading includes a solid example (complete with calculations and graphics).

### 3.9.4 Commodity Channel Index (CCI) is a metric that measures how (CCI)

The CCI assesses a security's current price level about its average price over a specific period. The moving average is frequently used to determine the average price level. Periods may be customized to provide the trader more control over when a binary option expires. The CCI effectively detects new trends and severe overbought/oversold circumstances inequities.

Day traders often use it for short-term trading and may be combined with other indicators like oscillators. "Price" is the asset's current price, "MA" is the asset's moving average, and "D" is the normal deviation from that average in the formula below. The commencement of a strong upswing is indicated by high readings over +100. The start of a significant downturn is indicated by values below -100. The CCI is calculated using the following formula:

$$CCI = \frac{Price - MA}{0.015 \times D}$$

**where:**

$Price$ = asset's current price

$MA$ = moving average of asset's price

$D$ = normal deviation from moving average

### 3.9.5 Oscillator Stochastic

In an interview, Dr. George Lane, the Stochastic Oscillator's originator, explained that "it tracks the pace or momentum of price." The momentum usually changes direction before the price." This crucial underlying element identifies severe occurrences of overbuying and overselling, allowing for identifying bullish and bearish phase reversals. The intersection of percent K and percent D values denotes the start of a transaction. Although a 14-day term is the most common, binary options traders may use whatever duration they like.

$$\%K = 100 \left( \frac{C - L14}{H14 - L14} \right)$$

**where:**

C = most recent closing price

L14 = low of 14 previous trading sessions

H14 = highest price traded during same 14-day p

$\%D = 3$ period moving average of $\%K$

Overbought levels are over 80, while oversold levels are below 20.

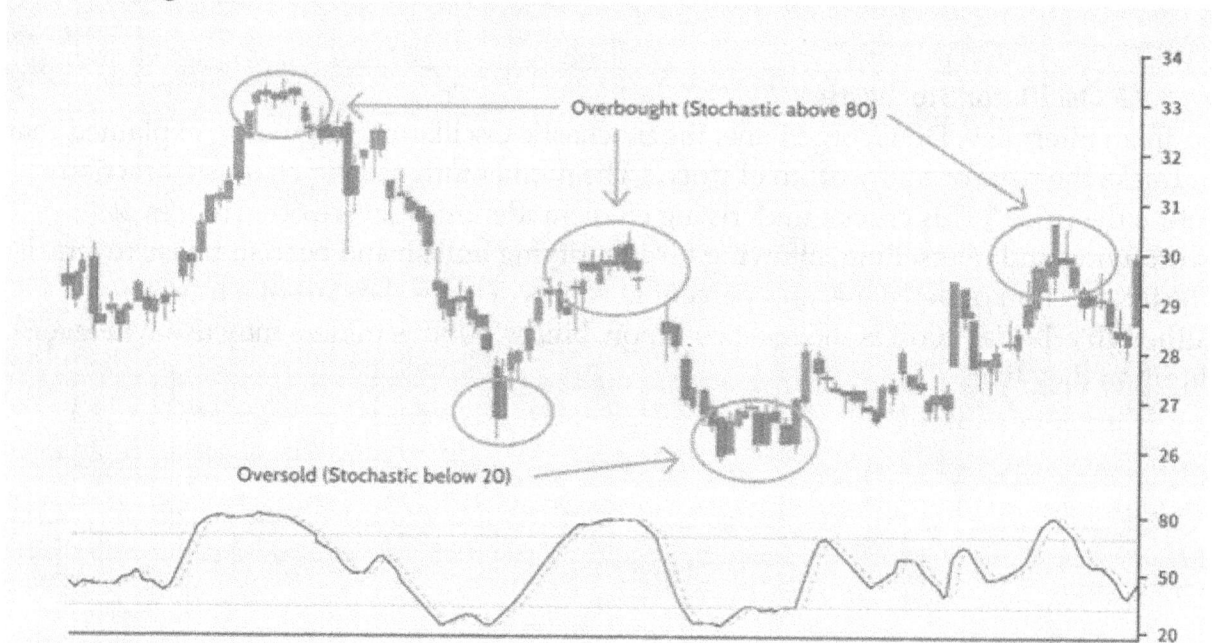

**3.9.6 Bollinger Bands are a kind of band that is used to describe**

Bollinger bands are a useful tool for capturing one component of volatility. They recognize upper and lower levels as dynamically created bands based on a security's previous price changes.

The most often used numbers for top and bottom bands are 12 for a simple moving average and two for a standard deviation.

The bands' contraction and expansion represent reversal indications, which assist traders in choosing optimal binary options positions. If the current market price is above the top band, it is considered overbought. Overselling is indicated when the current market price is lower than the bottom range.

Correctly anticipating the longevity of a trend over a certain time is a problem in binary options trading. For example, a trader may take the correct position for an index, forecasting that it would reach 1,250 by the conclusion of five hours, but the level was reached in the first two hours. Suppose the trader intends to maintain the position until expiration. In that case, constant monitoring is required for the next three hours, or a planned strategy (such as squaring off the position) should be performed once the level is achieved.

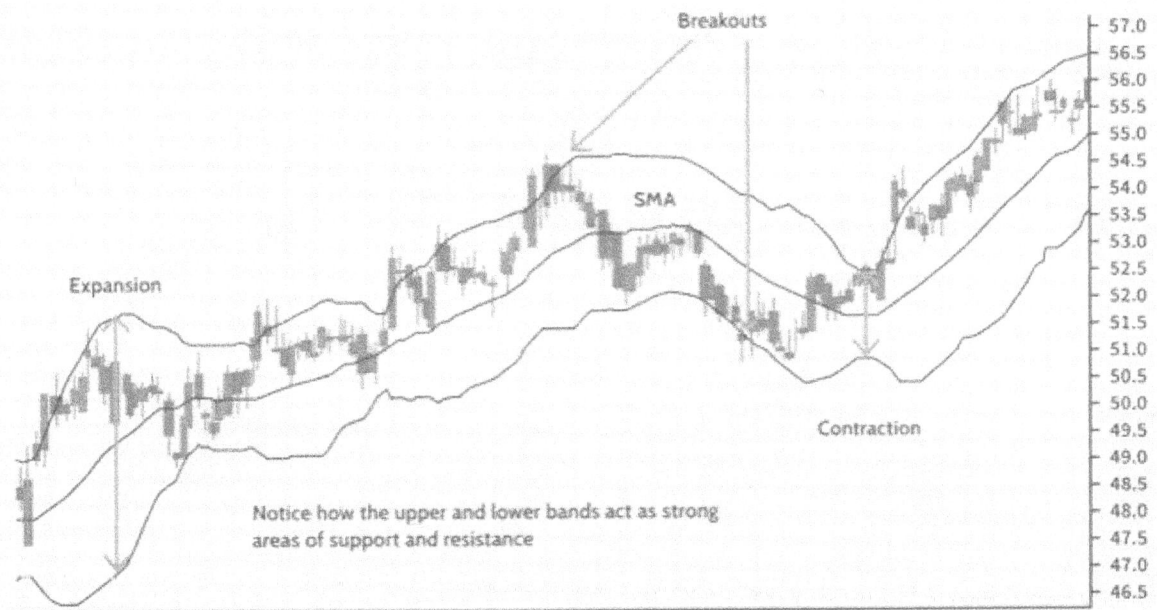

### 3.9.7 Final Thoughts

The above-mentioned technical indicators should be utilized to make timely decisions while constantly monitoring. Technical indicators have several drawbacks, including the fact that their conclusions and computations are dependent on historical data, which may lead to erroneous indications. For high-risk, high-return assets like binary options, traders should use prudence while doing rigorous back testing and thorough research.

### 3.9.8 Pivot Points

Traders on stock and commodities exchanges employ pivot points. They're computed using prior trading sessions' high, low, and closing prices, and they're used to forecast support and resistance levels for the current or forthcoming session. Traders may use these support and resistance levels to calculate entry and exit positions, as well as stop-loss and profit targets.

### 3.9.9 Pivot Points and How to Calculate Them

The five-point approach is the most frequent technique for finding pivot points out various options. This approach considers the previous day's high, low, and close, as well as two support and two resistance levels (for a total of five price points). The following are the equations:

$$\text{Pivot Point} = \frac{(\text{Previous High} + \text{Previous Low} + \text{Previous Close})}{3}$$

$$\text{Support 1 (S1)} = (\text{Pivot Point} * 2) - \text{Previous High}$$

$$\text{Support 2 (S2)} = \text{Pivot Point} - (\text{Previous High} - \text{Previous Low})$$

$$\text{Resistance 1 (R1)} = (\text{Pivot Point} * 2) - \text{Previous Low}$$

$$\text{Resistance 2 (R2)} = \text{Pivot Point} + (\text{Previous High} - \text{Previous Low})$$

Use the high, low, and close from the day's typical trading hours for equities that trade only during particular day hours.

Pivot points are often determined in 24-hour markets, such as the forex market, where the currency is transacted, utilizing New York closing time (4 p.m. EST) on a 24-hour cycle. Because the GMT is widely utilized in forex trading, some traders choose to finish a trading session at 23:59 GMT and initiate a new session at 00:00 GMT.

While it's common to use data from the previous day to create pivot points for the following day, it's also feasible to utilize data from the previous week to create pivot points for the next week. Swing traders and day traders might benefit from this to a lesser degree.

### 3.9.10 Alternative Techniques

The addition of the opening price in the calculation is another typical modification of the five-point system:

$$\text{Pivot Point} = \frac{(\text{Today's opening}+\text{Yesterday's High}+\text{Yesterday's Low}+\text{Yesterday's Close})}{4}$$

The opening price is now included in the calculation. The supports and resistances may then be computed using the modified pivot point in the same way as the five-point approach.

Tom DeMark, the creator and CEO of DeMARK Analytics created yet another pivot-point system.

The following rules apply to this system:

| Condition | Calculation | Tomorrow's Projections |
|---|---|---|
| Today's Close < Today's Open | Today's high + today's low + today's close + today's low = X | High = X/2 - today's low Low = X/2 - today's high |
| Today's Close > Today's Open | Today's high + today's low + today's close + today's high = X | High = X/2 - today's low Low = X/2 - today's high |
| Today's Close = Today's Open | Today's high + today's low + today's close + today's close = X | High = X/2 - today's low Low = X/2 - today's high |

As you can see, there are several pivot-point systems to choose from.

While learning how to compute pivot points is vital for understanding what you're working with, most charting programs do it for us. Simply add the pivot-point indicators to your chart and choose your preferred parameters.

### 3.9.11 Using and Interpreting Pivot Points

When calculating it, the pivot point is the major support and resistance. That indicates that the most significant price change is likely at this price. The other support and thrust levels are less powerful, but they can still cause big price changes.

There are two methods to employ pivot points. The first step is to establish the market's general trend. The market is bullish if the pivot point price is broken upward. It's bearish if the price declines through the pivot point.

The second way to enter and leave the markets is to employ pivot point price levels. A trader may, for example, place a limit order to purchase 100 shares if the price breaks through a barrier level. A trader might also place a stop loss at or around a support level.

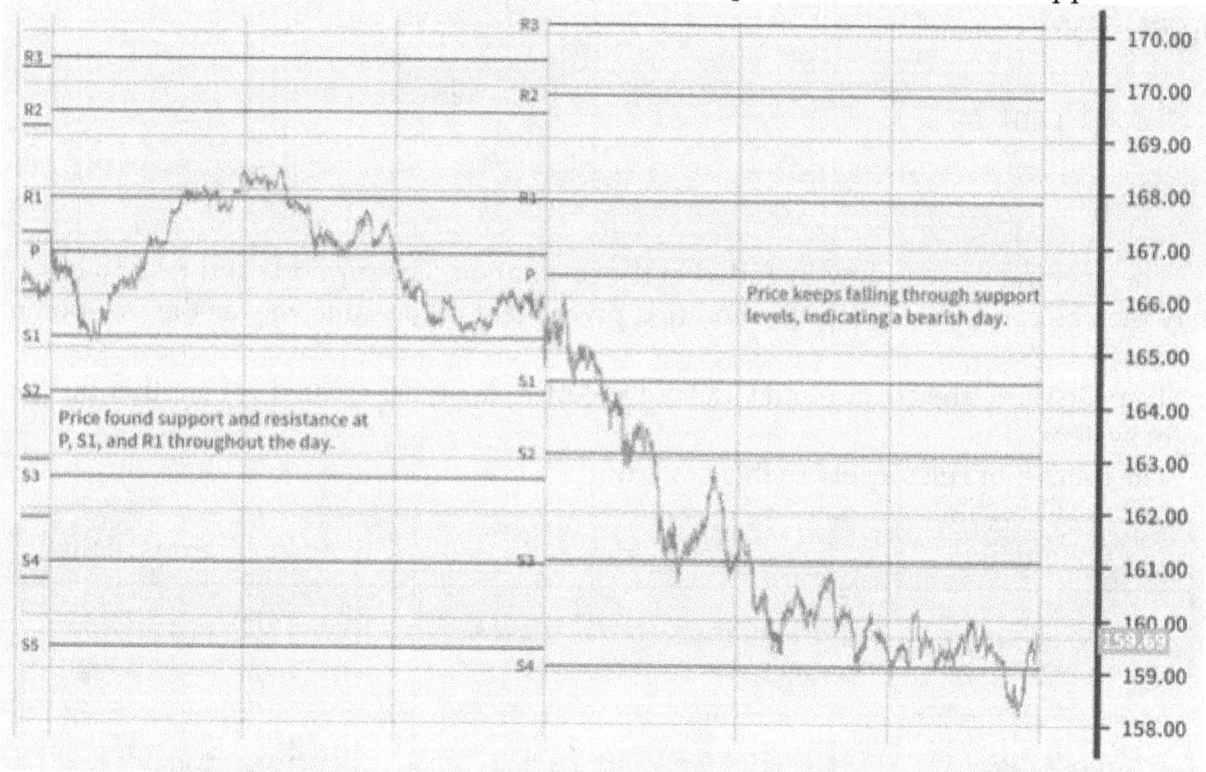

Price found support and resistance at P, S1, and R1 throughout the day.

Price keeps falling through support levels, indicating a bearish day.

While the levels seem to be quite excellent at anticipating price movement at times, they also appear to have not been affected at all at other times. Profits are unlikely to come from depending just on one signal, as with any other technical instrument.

The trader's ability to properly employ a pivot point method with other technical analyses is critical to its success. Other technical indicators include the MACD, candlestick patterns, and a moving average to determine trend direction. The more good indicators there are for a transaction, the more likely it will succeed.

# 3.10 Rules to Follow When Using Technical Analysis

Many investors evaluate companies based on their fundamentals, such as sales, valuation, or industry trends, but fundamentals aren't necessarily reflected in market pricing. Technical analysis examines past data, primarily price and volume, to forecast price moves.

It employs approaches such as statistical analysis and behavioral economics to assist traders and investors in navigating the gap between real value and market pricing. Technical analysis may assist traders in predicting what is most likely to happen based on previous data. Most investors make judgments based on both technical and fundamental research.

### 3.10.1 Select the Correct Approach

The top-down technique and the bottom-up approach are the two most common approaches to technical analysis. Short-term traders often use a top-down method, whereas long-term investors use a bottom-up one. Aside from that, there are five basic stages to getting started with technical analysis.

### Top-Down

The top-down strategy is a macroeconomic study that considers the whole economy before concentrating on specific assets. In the case of equities, a trader would initially focus on economies, then sectors, and last firms. Traders who use this strategy are more concerned with short-term profits than long-term values. A trader, for example, may be looking for equities that have broken out from their 50-day moving average as a buying opportunity.

### Bottom-Up

Instead of taking a macroeconomic picture, the bottom-up strategy concentrates on individual stocks. It entails looking for probable entry and exit opportunities in a stock that looks to be fundamentally intriguing. For example, an investor may come across a cheap stock in a downtrend and utilize technical analysis to pinpoint a certain entry moment when the price is likely to bottom out. They look for value in their selections and plan to keep their transactions for the long haul.

Aside from these factors, various kinds of traders may want to use other methods of technical analysis. Simple trend lines and volume indicators may be used by day traders, while chart patterns and technical indicators may be preferred by swing or position traders. Traders using automated algorithms may have different needs, such as using a mix of volume and technical indicators to make decisions.

### 3.10.2 Develop a trading system or choose a strategy

The first stage is to come up with a trading strategy or method. A rookie trader, for example, may choose to use a moving average crossover technique, in which they watch two moving averages (50-day and 200-day) on a single stock price movement.

If the short-term 50-day moving average crosses over the long-term 200-day moving average, it signals an upward market price and a buy signal for this approach. A sell signal is a polar opposite.

### 3.10.3 Determine the value of the securities

Not all equities or assets are suitable for the technique above, best suited to highly liquid and volatile stocks rather than illiquid or steady ones. In this example, alternative stocks or contracts may also need different parameter selections, such as 15-day and 50-day moving averages.

### 3.10.4 Locate a Reputable Brokerage

Find a trading account that supports the security you want to invest in (e.g., common stock, penny stock, futures, options, etc.). It should provide the necessary capability for tracking and monitoring the chosen technical indicators while being cost-effective to prevent eroding earnings. A simple account using moving averages on candlestick charts will suffice for the method above.

### 3.10.5. Keep track of your trades and keep an eye on them.

Depending on their technique, traders may want varying degrees of functionality. Day traders, for example, will want a margin account with Level II quotations and market maker visibility. However, a basic account may be preferred as a less expensive choice in our scenario.

### 3.10.6 Make use of extra software or tools

Other characteristics may be required to get peak performance. Some traders may need mobile notifications or mobile trading, while others may use automated trading systems to make transactions on their behalf.

### 3.10.7 Risk Factors and Recommendations

- Trading may be difficult, but completing your study beyond the criteria mentioned earlier is crucial. Other important factors to consider are:
- Understanding the basis behind the technical analysis and the logic that underpins it.
- Trading methods are back-tested to evaluate how well they might have done in the past.
- Before investing real money, you should practice trading on a demo account.
- To prevent expensive failures and surprises, be mindful of the limits of technical analysis.
- When it comes to scalability and future needs, be smart and adaptable.
- Requesting a free trial to test the features of a trading account.
- Starting small and increasing as you acquire experience is a good idea.

### 3.10.8 Final Thoughts

Many investors use both fundamental and technical research when making investing choices since technical analysis helps fill in information gaps. Traders and investors may increase their long-term risk-adjusted returns by learning technical analysis. Still, it's critical to understand and apply these strategies before investing real money to prevent expensive errors.

# CHAPTER 4

# STRATEGIES FOR OPTIONS TRADING

## 4.1 Strategy for Selling Covered Calls

We'll look at a trading method that's a great way for novices to get started selling options. Covered calls are the name of this approach. By covered, we mean that you have an asset that compensates you for the possibility of the underlying equities being sold. To put it another way, you already own stock shares. What's the point of writing a call option on equities you already own? The idea behind this technique is that you don't anticipate the stock price to change much throughout the life of the options contract, but you do want to make money in the near term by collecting premiums. It may help you establish a short-term revenue stream; but, you must properly plan your calls.

Setting up covered calls is a low-risk strategy that can help you learn about many facets of options trading. While it's unlikely to turn you into a productive worker overnight, it's a great method to master the tools of the trade.

### 4.1.1 A long position is required for covered calls

To construct a covered call, you must hold at least 100 shares in one underlying equity. You'll be providing prospective purchasers the opportunity to acquire these shares from you when you establish a call. Of course, the plan is only to sell when the price is high, but the main purpose is to acquire the premium revenue stream.

The premium is a non-refundable one-time cost. If a buyer buys your call option and pays the premium, you get the money. Whatever happens after that, you get to keep the money. The contract will expire if the stock does not reach the strike price, and you may arrange a new call option on the same underlying shares. Of course, if the stock price rises over the strike price, the contract buyer will most likely exercise their right to purchase the shares. You'll still make money on the deal, but the danger is that you'll forego the opportunity to make as much money as you might have.

A covered call option with a strike price of $67 is written. Assume the stock rises to $90 per share due to some unanticipated event. Your call option buyer will be able to acquire the shares from you for $67. So you've made a $2 profit each share. You did, however, lose out on the opportunity to sell the shares for a profit of $35 a share. Instead, the investor who acquired the call option from you will sell the shares on the open market for the real spot price, and they will profit.

However, you haven't truly lost anything. You've earned the premium and made a little profit on your stock sales.

The danger of the stocks rising to a substantially higher price than the strike price always remains, but if you do your research, you'll be providing equities that you don't anticipate to fluctuate much in price throughout the term of the call. So, let's pretend the price merely went up to $68.

The buyer could execute their option because the price was higher than the strike price.

In such a situation, you're still losing out on some profit you might have made otherwise, but it's just a tiny amount, and the premium isn't considered.

If the stock price does not rise over the strike price throughout the contract's life, you retain the premium and the shares. Whatever happens, the premium is yours to keep. In most cases, a covered call will be a win-win scenario for you.

### 4.1.2 Covered Calls are a Risk-Free Investment Strategy

A covered call strategy is referred to be a "neutral" approach. Covered calls are created for stocks in a portfolio where the investor only expects minor movements during the contract term. Furthermore, covered calls will be used on equities that investors anticipate to keep for a long time. It's a strategy to make money on stocks when the investor anticipates the stock to remain relatively unchanged in price and hence has little profit potential from selling.

### 4.1.3 A Covered Call Example

Let's pretend you possess 100 Acme Communications shares. It is now selling for $40 per share. Nobody expects the stock to move much in the next months, but you believe Acme Communications has significant long-term growth potential as an investor. You sell a call option on Acme Communications with a strike price of $43 to earn some money. Assume the premium is $0.78 and the call option is three months.

You'll get a total premium payment of $0.78 x 100 = $78 for 100 shares.

You keep the $78 regardless of what happens.

Let's imagine the stock decreases a little in price during the following three months, never approaching the strike price, and it ends up trading at $39 a share after the time.

The options contract will be worthless when it expires. The buyer of the options contract is left with nothing. It's a win-win scenario for you.

You've earned an additional $78 per 100 shares, and after the contract, you still own your shares.

Let's pretend that the stock's value rises a little. Over time, it rises to $42, then $42.75, before falling to $41.80 by the options contract expires. You're in a much better position in this situation. The strike price of $43 was never achieved in this scenario. Thus the call option buyer was again left out in the cold. On the other hand, you retain the $78 premium and your stock shares.

You're a lot better off this time since the shares have grown in value, so it's a win-win scenario for you, even if it's a terrible one for the poor individual who bought your call.

Unfortunately, there is a chance that the stock price will surpass the strike price before the contract expires. If that's the case, you'll have to sell the shares. However, you still find yourself in a situation that isn't too horrible. You didn't lose any cash, but you did miss out on a possible profit. You will still get the $78 premium, as well as the proceeds from the selling of 100 shares at the strike price of $43.

A covered call is practically risk-free since you never lose money, even if the stock price jumps, indicating that you missed out on an opportunity. You may reduce this risk by carefully selecting equities for a covered call option. For example, if you own shares in a pharmaceutical business that is expected to announce a cancer cure in two months, you shouldn't utilize those shares for a covered call. A better bet is a firm with stronger long-term possibilities but is unlikely to go anywhere in the next few months.

### 4.1.4 What steps should you take to make a covered call

You'll need 100 shares of stock to establish a covered call. While you don't want to take a chance on a stock that is expected to rise shortly, you also don't want to buy a complete stinker. Someone is always eager to purchase anything if the price is right. However, you want to choose a good stock to earn a good premium.

You begin by going to your brokerage's website and searching up the stock. When you check for stocks online, you may look at their "option chain," which provides information from a table on premiums available for calls on the stock. These are included under the bid price section. A call contract comprises 100 shares. However, the bid price is stated per share. If your bid price is $1.75, the real premium you'll get is $1.75 multiplied by 100 = $175.

It's worth noting that the larger the premium, the farther away the expiry date is. A reasonable rule of thumb is to choose an expiration date two to three months from now. Remember that the longer you wait, the larger the risk, since the probabilities of the stock price exceeding the strike price and forcing you to sell the shares rise.

With the premium you wish to charge, you have a choice (pun intended). You can theoretically set whatever price you desire. Of course, you'll need a customer willing to pay that amount to earn any money. Looking at the prices, people are now demanding call options on this stock is a more acceptable technique. It may be done by looking at the asking price for the stock's call options. By checking the bid prices, you can also discover what prices buyers are now offering. You may just set your pricing to a bid price already out there for a quick sale. You may place the order and then wait for someone to come along and purchase your call option at the asking price if you want to go a little higher.

Select "sell to open" to sell a covered call.

## 4.2 The Advantages of Covered Calls

A covered call is a low-risk investment. In the worst-case scenario, you'll lose your stock but make a tiny profit, which is less than you might have gained if you hadn't placed the call contract and just sold your stock. You do, however, receive the premium.

A covered call is a strategy for generating money from your portfolio via premiums.

It's a decent technique to produce income without incurring much risk if you don't foresee any market movements in the short future and want to retain the stock for a long time.

## 4.3 The Dangers of Covered Calls

If you're optimistic about a company and your predictions are met, and the price spikes, covered calls might be dangerous. In that situation, you've exchanged a modest amount of premium income with a voluntary strike price limit for the potential gain you might have had if you just kept the stock and sold it at a high price.

If the stock price falls while you are still receiving the premium, the stock will be worthless until it recovers over time.

You should avoid using a call option on equities that you believe will see a significant downturn in the future months. Instead of writing a covered call in this scenario, you should just sell the stocks and accept your losses. Alternatively, you may keep the stocks and wait for them to recover in the long run.

# 4.4 Stepping Up a Tier

A contingency order is one way to reduce risk while increasing the chances in your favor. A contingency order works similarly to a stop order, except that the price trigger depends on the stock rather than the option. Let's use our PQR put sell as an example and construct a condition where we would exit the option position in an offsetting transaction if PQR shares (initially at 100 when we implemented the trade) fell below 90.

Our contingency is a fee of $90. The trigger, or contingency, is struck if PQR shares drop below 90, and we quit the PQR put. We leave when the PQR shares, not the price of the PQR put, reach a certain level. Our loss would be minimized in this case.

What if PQR shares gapped lower, posing a problem? Let's assume the stock dropped to 91 before plunging to 70 in a Flash Crash. Although this is exceedingly implausible, it is not out of the realm of possibility. It's happened before. Such a catastrophe would be catastrophic and unavoidable.

Using a spread might be a better approach... a better strategy. You may establish an option spread that lowers risk while increasing the likelihood of profit by combining option purchases and short sells.

This spread technique is ideal for index options and index-based ETF options (such as SPY). The liquidity is excellent, and transaction costs are low. True probabilities are also quite simple to compute.

By the way, the method we discussed is referred to as a credit spread. Because you get paid at the start of the deal when you employ a credit spread, it is termed a credit spread. A credit spread is a technique in which you sell one option and purchase another that is more out-of-the-money at the same time.

As an example, imagine you're a stock index trader. You choose to trade an ETF version of a stock index rather than a cash-settled index. The ETF you're tracking is now trading for $150. You would sell a 140 put and purchase a 135 put if you were bullish. You'd win as long as the ETF remained over 140. In other words, if the ETF rose in value, you would profit. You'd earn money even if the ETF didn't move. You would gain money if the ETF decreased by 5%. You'd still earn money if it dropped 6%. The ETF may drop 7% or more, depending on the magnitude of the credit you got, and you could still earn money. That's why the chances are so good: there's only one scenario in which you lose, and even then, it's only a little loss7.

A credit spread with a negative tendency is also an option. In this case, you might sell the 160 call and purchase the 165 call simultaneously. In this case, if the index fell, you would profit. You'd earn money even if the market stayed steady. Even if the index rose 5%, you'd still gain money. If the index rose by more than 7%, you would lose money. The chances are wonderful when selling a put credit spread since there is only one scenario in which you lose, and even then, the loss potential is quite restricted.

Combining a call credit spread with a put credit spread is unique.

Remember how we said earlier that the stock market seldom moves more than 5% up or down in a month? You can use choices to put that inclination to work for you. You may make money as the market trades up and down in a broad range by simply selling a call credit spread and a put credit spread at the same time. According to history, this method should generate money more than 80% of the time.

Based on historical data, even higher outcomes may be attained in the correct market.

When you use one spread style, you get results like this. To generate money and manage risk, you may use an almost infinite variety of techniques and option combinations.

## 4.5 Buying Call Strategy

You pay the option premium in return for the right to acquire shares at a defined price (strike price) on or before a specific date when you buy a call (expiration date). When investors are optimistic about a stock or other investment, they often purchase calls because they provide leverage.

Let's say ABC Company is valued at $50. The stock's one-month at-the-money call option costs $3. Would you rather pay $5,000 for 100 ABC shares or $300 for a call option that pays out based on the stock's closing price one month from now? Take a look at the visual representations of the two situations below.

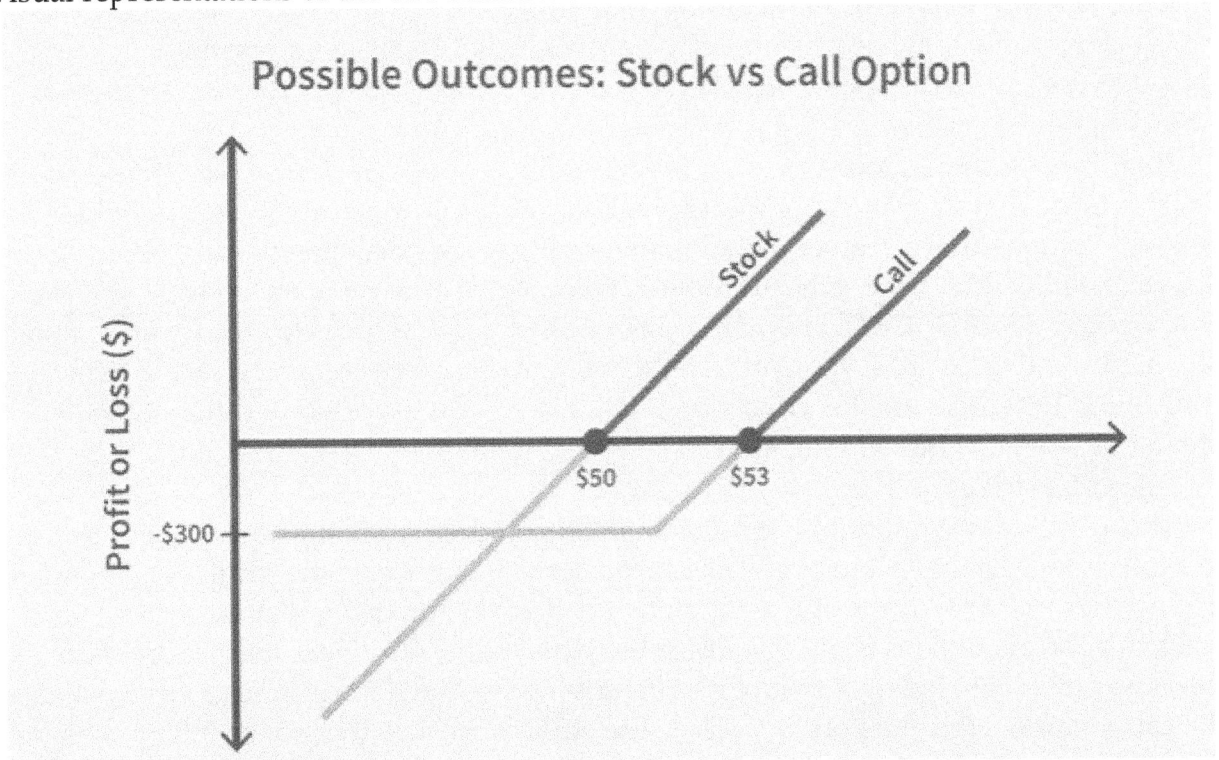

Possible Outcomes: Stock vs Call Option

As you can see, each investment has a distinct payback. While purchasing the stock requires a $5,000 investment, buying a call option allows you to own an identical number of shares for just $300. Also, the stock trade's breakeven price is $50 per share, while the option trade's breakeven price is $53 per share (not factoring in commissions or fees).

While both investments have infinite upside potential in the month after purchase, the risk of loss differs dramatically. For example, although the maximum possible loss on the option is $300, the maximum potential loss on a stock purchase is the whole $5,000 original investment if the stock price falls to zero.

### 4.5.1 Closing the Position

Investors may either sell their call holdings back to the market or exercise them, in which case they must give payment to the counter-party who sold them the calls (and receive the shares in exchange).

Let's imagine that the stock was trading at $55 towards the one-month expiry in our scenario. You may sell your call for about $500 ($5 100 shares) in this situation, giving you a net profit of $200 ($500 less the $300 premium).

You might also have the call exercised, which would obligate you to pay $5,000 ($50 100 shares) and require the counter-party who sold you the call to deliver the shares. The profit would be $200 with this strategy ($5,500 - $5,000 - $300 = $200). It's worth noting that the reward from exercising or selling the call is the same $200 net profit.

### 4.5.2 Considerations for Call Option

When opposed to buying the underlying stock, buying calls requires more considerations. Assuming you've picked on a stock for which to purchase calls, there are a few things to consider:

### Premium Outlay Amount

This is the first stage in the procedure. In most circumstances, an investor would choose to purchase a call rather than the underlying stock since the call has a lesser financial outlay. Using the same example as before, if you have $1,500 to invest, you can only purchase 30 ABC Co. shares at the current stock price of $50. However, based on the one-month call price of $3, you would be able to purchase five contracts (each contract controlling 100 shares and hence costing $300), giving you the option— but not the obligation—to purchase 500 shares at $50.

### Price of a strike

This is one of two important option variables to choose from, the other being the time to expiry. Because the striking price has such a large influence on the result of an options trade, you should conduct some research before deciding on the best strike price. The basic rule for call options is that the lower the strike price, the bigger the call premium (because you obtain the right to buy the underlying stock at a lower price). The smaller the call premium, the more out of pocket. The strike price is at the money in this example, meaning it equals the stock's current price of $50.

Another important element is the time before the product expires. When it comes to options, the longer the period to expiry, the larger the option premium. A balance between time and cost must be made when determining the time to expiry. The third Friday of each month is when options contracts normally expire.

### Contracts with option clauses

You'll have a good notion of the call premium after you've decided on the strike price and the period to expiry. With $1,500 to invest and each one-month $50 call option costing $300, you must determine whether to purchase five contracts for the whole amount available or three or four contracts and hold some cash in reserve.

---

Option order type: Option prices may be highly volatile, being a derivative of stock prices. You'll need to select whether to use a market order or a limit order for your calls.

**What is the maximum amount of money I may lose by purchasing a call option**

The maximum loss for a call buyer equals the price paid for the call.

### 4.5.3 What are some of the disadvantages of purchasing call options

One disadvantage is that both critical variables—the strike price and the time to expiration—must be correct. The call will expire worthless if the underlying stock never moves higher than your strike price before expiration or if it climbs higher than the strike price but only after options expiration. Another downside of purchasing options, whether calls or puts, is that their value depreciates over time as the expiry date approaches, a process known as time decay.

### 4.5.4 Is it wise to execute my call option if it is in the money and the expiry date is still a few weeks away

No, it would be unwise to do so in the vast majority of circumstances. Early exercise would prevent the investor from capturing the time value of the call option, resulting in a lesser gain than if the call option were sold. Early exercise makes sense only in certain circumstances, such as when the option is deeply in the money and about to expire since the time value is low in this situation.

### 4.5.5 Should I purchase a call option on a stock with high volatility if I believe in its long-term prospects

Your call option might be rather costly if the stock is very volatile. Furthermore, if the stock does not move above the strike price, the call may expire without execution. You could be better off purchasing the stock rather than a call option on it if you are enthusiastic about its long-term prospects.

The Bottom Line Trading calls may be a good method to increase your stock or other security exposure without committing a lot of money. Funds and big investors often utilize such calls because they enable them to control enormous volumes of stock with very little cash.

# 4.6 Understanding Time Value and Volatility

As an options trader, you must understand the factors that influence an option's pricing and the ins and outs of putting the correct strategy in place. A stock trader who is used to anticipating future stock price movement may believe that transitioning to options trading is simple, but it is not.

An options trader must deal with three moving parameters: the underlying stock's price, the time factor, and volatility. Any of these variables will impact the cost of the choice.

The premium is the price of an option, and it is calculated per share. The option seller gives a tip and then offers the buyer any rights to the option. The buyer is the one who pays the seller for the knowledge, and they have the option of exercising this privilege or letting the chance pass them by with no value. Whether the buyer exercises the option or not, the buyer is obligated to pay the premium, which implies the seller will retain the tip in the future regardless of what happens.

Let's have a look at a basic example. A buyer paid a seller for the right to acquire 100 shares of company ABC at a strike price of $60. The contract is set to end on June 19th. The buyer exercises the option if the option position becomes lucrative. The buyer might simply let the contract expire if it does not seem to be profitable. The vendor then keeps the premium.

An option premium's intrinsic and temporal value is two sides of the same coin. The difference between the strike and stock prices may be used to calculate an option's intrinsic value. The stock price minus the strike price is the stock price for a call option. It is the strike price minus the stock price for a put option.

Multiple factors, such as the underlying stock price, volatility, exercise price, time to expiry, and interest rate, must be considered to value an option, at least theoretically. These characteristics will give you a good assessment of an option's fair value, which you may use in your plan to maximize profits. Only the time and volatility variables will be discussed in depth. The fundamental purpose of option pricing is to determine the likelihood that a given option will be 'in the money or exercised before it expires.

Underlying stock price fluctuations directly influence the value of puts and calls. For example, if the price of a stock increases, the call value should also climb since you may buy the underlying stock at a lower price than the market, as long as the price drop input is there. When the stock price falls, the value of put options should rise, while the cost of call options should fall since the put option holder has the opportunity to sell the shares at above-market prices. The striking price or exercise price is the pre-determined price you may sell or acquire. The option is deemed 'in the money if the strike price offers you the benefit of selling or purchasing the stock at a price that gives you an instant profit.

Now that we've covered the underlying stock price and strike price, we can move on to the other two primary elements that might influence an option's pricing: time and volatility.

# 4.7 Time

Time is a valuable commodity. This aphorism remains true even in the world of options trading. As a result, knowing how the Greek theta works are critical and impact option pricing. The Greek letter theta reflects the influence of time decay on the value of a chance, if you recall. As the contract expiry date approaches, all options, call or put, lose weight, but the value loss rate of an option contract depends on the length of time before it expires.

The irrelevant section is the only component of an option's value impacted by time decay. An "in the money" option will have the same inherent value until the contract expires. For example, a stock that trades at $3, a call for a 30-strike price, will keep its intrinsic value of $3 until it expires. Even yet, any contract with a value of more than $3 is deemed irrelevant and influenced by time decay.

Because theta indicates the loss of value through time, it usually has a negative value. And, since time is irreversible, it merely slows down and never stops or reverses. Assume theta is -0.28; the accompanying option contract will lose $0.28 in value per day.

Theta, on the other hand, changes throughout time. Assume that the price of a stock stays stable, and a $2.75 'out of the money option with a -0.15 theta will be worth $2.60 the next day. If stock prices stay steady, the theta can only be set to -0.12, implying that the option's cost will fall to $2.48 the following day. While the option is still 'out of the money,' its value will steadily approach zero.

You should also keep in mind that theta's influence gets more noticeable as the expiry date approaches. Within the last few days, before the contract expires, you can expect a dramatic acceleration of the time decay.

Extrinsically, options that are 'at the money' have the most value.

As a result, the thetas for these parameters are set to the maximum. Because 'at the money options' have lower extrinsic values, deep options 'in the money or 'out of the money have lower thetas. And the lower the extrinsic value of an option, the less it will lose over time.

Short alternatives are the only way for the theta position to be advantageous.

Because short option positions operate best in a steady market, this is the case.

Large swings in either direction harm option positions or only time will aid as time passes. Other techniques, such as neutral strategies, such as the long butterfly, gain from the passage of time. The shorter time left before the contract expires, the less likely the underlying stock will increase or fall and enter the unprofitable territory.

There will always be a trade-off between market movement and time for any option position. It isn't easy to have the best of both worlds simultaneously. If the passage of time is beneficial to your option position, the price movement will be detrimental. The same is true in the other direction. Returning to our Greeks, theta's inverse is gamma (or price movement). A negative gamma will result from a favorable theta position (one that benefits from the passage of time). A positive gamma will result from a negative theta position (function adversely impacted by the passage of time).

# 4.8 Volatility

Volatility impacts most investment forms to some extent, and as an options trader, you should be aware of how it influences option pricing. Volatility is defined as the propensity for anything to vary or alter considerably. Volatility, in general, refers to the rate at which the price of a financial item increases or decreases.

A financial instrument with minimal volatility has reasonably consistent pricing.

A high volatility financial instrument, on the other hand, is prone to large price movements in either direction. We assess financial market volatility in general. As a result, when the market becomes impossible to anticipate and prices fluctuate often and fast, the market is volatile.

Volatility has a big impact on the option price. Many novice options traders overlook the ramifications, resulting in significant financial losses.

Before engaging in any transaction, including options trading, it is important to understand its volatility. Volatility is a key aspect in determining how options are evaluated and priced. Historical and implied volatility are the two forms of volatility that matter.

## 4.8.1 Volatility in History

The price of the underlying option is measured by historical or statistical volatility, which is based on actual and genuine data. For the time being, we'll refer to it as HV. HV indicates how quickly the stock price has changed. The greater the HV, the more the stock price has fluctuated over time. As a result, a stock with a high HV is more likely to fluctuate in price, at least theoretically. It's more of a hint to future movement than a firm commitment.

On the other hand, a low HV may imply that the stock price hasn't changed much but consistently moves in one direction.

HV can be used to forecast how much a security's price will fluctuate given how quickly it has changed in the past, but it cannot be used to anticipate a trend.

HV is measured over a certain period, such as a week, month, or year, and maybe calculated in various methods.

## 4.8.2 Implied Volatility

Options traders should be mindful of implied volatility, often known as IV. Unlike HV, which gauges a security's previous volatility, IV predicts future volatility.

IV is a forecast of how quickly and how much the stock price will fluctuate in the future. When determining an option's value, many new traders concentrate on profitability (the difference between the strike price and the stock price) and contract expiry, but IV is also important.

The IV of an option may be calculated by considering elements such as the stock and strike prices, the period to expiry, the current interest rate, and the HV. Because the IV of an option might indicate how much the stock will vary in price, the price rises as the IV rises. Because, theoretically, you make more money when the underlying stock price fluctuates dramatically. Even if the stock price stays the same, the value of an option might vary, and it is generally due to its IV.

For example, ABC is set to produce a new product, and rumors circulate disclosing it soon. Because there is a strong likelihood of large volatility in the underlying stock price, the options' IV for stock ABC might be quite high. The announcement may be accurate, and the stock price may rise; nevertheless, the audience may be dissatisfied with the new product, which may fall rapidly. The stock price may not change in this circumstance since investors will be waiting for the news announcement before purchasing or selling stocks. Extrinsic value for both puts and calls will rise as a result, rather than the stock price moving. It's one of the ways IV may influence option price.

If you believe a stock's price will rise considerably due to the news, you may buy at-the-money call options to maximize the likely profits. There would have been large gains in the call options' intrinsic value if ABC had announced and was favorably accepted, prompting stock prices to skyrocket.

# 4.9 How to Buy and Sell Puts

Let's speak about how to purchase and sell puts. On the other hand, puts enable you to sell the stock you own or the underlying commodity that underpins it all. There are various reasons individuals would want to purchase or sell puts, and we'll go over what they are, how to do it, and the benefits of doing so here.

### 4.9.1 What is the difference between buying and selling puts

Selling/buying puts effectively allows someone to purchase a stock for a certain price.

When you sell a put option, you're essentially selling the right to someone else to purchase that stock at a certain price.

When you purchase a put option, you're allowing someone to buy your stock at a certain price, but you're forced to sell it.

So, let's assume you will purchase a put option on that stock for a particular amount of money. You can place that option on the table and then wait for it to fall, at which point you may exercise it. Perhaps you'd want to invest in a reputable railroad firm. You observe that it's rising profits on this, and you decide to purchase the stock while it's maybe around 30. By purchasing a put option, you effectively require the seller to sell you the stock if it goes below $30.

You should use them in declining markets since you will make money if it falls rather than rises.

### 4.9.2 In this market, selling puts

The point is, if you want to sell puts, you should only do so if you're OK with owning the stock below it at the current price since you're effectively adopting the duty to purchase it if the individual decides to sell. As a result, you should only participate in transactions if the net price paid for the asset is favorable. It is the most crucial aspect of effectively selling puts in the markets you have. There are further reasons to sell it to the individual. You may also buy the security at a lower price than the current market price, but you'll want to be cautious if you decide to sell it.

### 4.9.3 Buying a Put as an Example

Let's get started purchasing these puts immediately. One thing to keep in mind is that commissions, taxes, margins, and other fees aren't included in any of these calculations for a reason. That begins to become a little more involved, so for now, we're just going through the basics of all the many methods you may purchase a put option. However, you should contact your tax expert or broker before entering.

So, let's assume you have firm A, which is now overvalued at $50 per share, and you decide to bet on a drop at this time by purchasing a put option for $35 per share for $2 per share, resulting in a "breakeven" price of $33 per share. Because you're taking the contract price of 35 minus the 2 to get $33, you can conclude this from simple arithmetic because each of them represents 100 separate shares. That totals $3500, and you'll have to pay $200 ahead for this (due to the options contract and the shares), after which you'll be able to join the transaction. Let's imagine the option contract is for August 2019, and you want to fast-forward and keep an eye on the market. A table of what may happen is shown below.

| Action of stock | What happens to you | Your return | Outlook |
|---|---|---|---|
| Soars all the way up to $60 | The option expires, becomes worthless, and you lose the $200 premium, but you're basically losing nothing else | (100%) | Okay |

| | | | |
|---|---|---|---|
| Falls slightly to $38 | Same thing happens, stock falls but you don't make a profit | (100%) | Okay |
| Drops all the way to $25 | You make some cash! 800 dollars to be exact ($35-25) and then the $2 premium | (800%) | Nice! |
| Drops to $0 (basically going bankrupt) | The ideal situation, and you'll get $3300 from it (0 at expiration, so 3500-200 from the premium) | (1500%) | Ideal! |

So, when you have a sinking ship in terms of stock, now is the greatest moment to utilize it. Otherwise, they're not worth your time, and it's best to avoid these stocks altogether since there's always the risk of losing money.

However, if the individual sells the stock and you cash in on it, you'll have more money and won't have to worry about the stock's burden.

If you opt to acquire it when it falls in value, you will effectively make money. You only want to do it while it's on the decline. You mustn't act on these sorts of possibilities until the appropriate period has passed.

That's all; purchasing put options is all there is to it, and you want to make sure it falls to the amount you want.

### 4.9.4 The dangers of it

In both circumstances, there are risks. They are hazardous because of the complexity of options, but you can greatly lower the risk if you understand how they operate. Put options, in particular, may be dangerous, particularly for the seller, who may have to pay more money to repurchase the option they previously had.

Another consideration, particularly for purchasers, is the breakeven point. Thus, let's say you bought a stock today for $46, and it was at $44, which is two points lower than it is now, so the purchase will be lucrative. But here's the thing: because of the charge for the option, you'll end up losing money. It would make the option worth $2, but you already paid $4 for it, so you'd be losing money.

But there's also the reality that if the option expires in the money, you'll get the correct stock straight away. You may not realize it, but they may be beneficial, particularly in plummeting markets when you know the market will recover.

If it goes higher in value, you'll have to pay a premium to gain the right to purchase it, which may be a couple of thousand dollars. When you decide to figure out your stock, be sure you understand what you're doing and how to correct it readily.

### 4.9.5 The Benefits of Purchasing Puts

If you want to protect yourself, buy options that offer you the opportunity to sell the stock at a certain price. So, let's assume you own this stock or have been eyeing one that will most likely decline and increase in the next months. There are such out there, and it's generally due to market lulls at the time. So you decide to purchase the available put, allowing you to sell the stock if the market rises to a greater level.

You're taking a risk here since the market may not rebound, but if you see a stock that has the potential to plummet, this might be a good one. You'll be able to obtain the goods at a lower price this way. After then, you may sell the stock again, and you have the legal right to sell it at the price you choose.

It effectively enables you to instill an additional sense of confidence in him, which is a wonderful little bonus for the one looking to sell it. Long puts are ideal for this, particularly if you intend to sell them.

Put options allow you to sell this asset at the current strike price. The seller must acquire these shares from the holder due to this. So, how does this assist? Let's imagine you purchase a stock for $20 and then compare it against another stock for $20 at the edge. You may exercise the options and lessen your losses if the price falls below 20 at any stage.

It may be beneficial, particularly if you're prepared to purchase an option and then sell it to prevent many problems.

### 4.9.6 Naked Puts

There are also naked puts, a more complex put option strategy that I wouldn't recommend attempting until you've mastered basic puts. The reason for this is that they are very dangerous.

However, what does it mean to trade an option naked? It doesn't imply you're going to the stock market in your underwear; rather, you're selling options without owning the underlying asset. For example, when you write a naked put, you're selling a put without owning the stock.

The simplest fundamental stock trading method is the covered call. This technique is a great place for newcomers to options trading since it enables them to use their present investing activity as a doorway to trading options. The covered call's concept is straightforward.

This method aims to keep your stock purchases' cost basis as low as possible.

Let's have a peek at the process.

### 4.9.7 Other Things to Think About

The time value incorporated into the option is the main money source in this method. Consider the following scenario: we keep the 1270 strike but change the expiry date. What premiums would we get if the strike dates were closer together than the one on October 25th?

The expiration of the calls on September 20th, which is less than a week away, will net you $0.19. You'll get $1.40 on September 27th. In October, things started to look up. We get $4.80 on October 4th.

Finally, we'll get $6.90 on October 11th and $9.91 on October 18th, which is roughly a week after our October 25th pick. As a consequence of the week difference, the premium drops from $16 to $9.91.

That's a 38 percent discount! Hopefully, you can understand where I'm coming from regarding the importance of time decay. It reduces gradually; therefore, you should use it as much as possible. Given that time decays exponentially, isn't it reasonable to choose an expiration date as far away as possible? So, let's see how this unfolds.

# 4.10 Understanding the Greeks

Only a few Greek letters—delta, gamma, theta, Vega, and Rho—are in the language of the ordinary options trader, with delta being the most helpful.

### 4.10.1 Delta

One of the things that makes delta so valuable is how simple it is to comprehend. As we discussed in Chapter 2, if you purchase an option and the underlying stock rapidly jumps in the desired direction, it's typically more beneficial (and lucrative) to resell the option rather than execute it. When the underlying stock changes by a single point, the delta measure tells you how much the price of your option is likely to move. Though the data offered by delta isn't without flaws, it might be a valuable reference point when attempting to assess an option's prospective profitability.

Deltas always have an absolute value between 0 and 1; traders sometimes omit the decimal place, referring to the option as having a 50 delta rather than a.5 delta. The delta of calls is always positive, whereas the delta of puts is always negative.

The delta for an option is usually offered, particularly on brokerage or exchange websites specializing in options trading, but it's also simple to compute. All you'll need are snapshots of both the stock's and option's values. Take, for example, a call option. Let's imagine the stock is trading at $30, and there's a call option with two months till expiry that's ATM (at the money), as well as a $30 call contract that can be acquired for $1 per share right now. When the stock rises in value, say to $32, the call option will also increase in value. (The call option is suddenly $2 in the money in this situation.) Let's assume the call option increases from $1 to $2 per share. Divide the change in the option price by the change in the stock price to get the option's delta. In this case, you get.5 by dividing 1 by 2. A "50 delta" is a term used to describe this situation.

Using this technique, you can understand why calculating the delta value of a put option always yields a negative amount. As the stock price rises, the value of the put option decreases, resulting in a negative delta value when you divide a negative number by a positive number or vice versa.

### 4.10.2 Preventing Common Frustrations with Delta

Purchasing an option and seeing the stock value increase $2 or even $3 in the "correct" direction only to discover that the option's value has scarcely moved is one of the things that irritates beginner-level options traders and may turn them off to options completely. Many newcomers to the options market may be tempted to the very low-cost, out-of-the-money option contracts with very little time remaining on them. You can acquire one of these contracts for $20, but it's unlikely that you'll earn any money from it. The reason for this is because, towards expiry, the delta value of out-of-the-money option contracts is close to zero. Even if the stock advances dramatically in the right direction, the option may not earn much value. Many of these OTM choices are the equivalents of a Hail Mary throw since they are so inexpensive and practically expired. You may avoid this difficulty by learning how to understand the delta value.

### 4.10.3 Gamma

The projected change in the delta value regarding a $1 change in the stock price is measured by gamma. Remember that the delta value changes during the life of an option, but the amount to which it does so depends on a variety of circumstances, including the closeness to the option's expiry date.

The idea of gamma risk is the most crucial thing for a beginner-level options trader to comprehend about the gamma meter. If your gamma level is high and you can profit or limit loss by selling or exercising your option, you should do so since the option's value might swiftly decrease.

Though professionals utilize gamma analysis, particularly in risk assessments, it's unnecessary to have a detailed grasp of applying this statistic when you're just getting started. The gamma metric's bottom line is that when gamma rises, the values of your options become more sensitive to fluctuations in the stock's price.

### 4.10.4 Theta

The price change of an option regarding a unit of time is measured by theta (usually a day). All other circumstances being equal, the closer an option approaches its expiry date, the less value it is likely to have. The theta metric measures how much this value fluctuates daily. As a result, theta has a negative value. In the world of options, this loss of value is known as "theta decay."

For a newcomer, it's important to know that theta decay reduces the value of an option at an ever-increasing pace. If you're thinking about selling an option with three weeks or less remaining on the contract, be aware that theta decay will significantly reduce the value of your option. Theta decay becomes more severe as you move near to your expiry date.

Edward Olmstead illustrates theta decay using basic square roots in his book Options for Beginners. "Theta for an at-the-money option varies inversely as the square root of the remaining time till expiry," he explains. That may seem to be a mouthful, but it becomes understandable when considered in the context of a real-life incident.

If you still can't get your brain around theta, simply remember that the time decay becomes more significant as the option approaches expiration.

However, keep in mind that theta is never the be-all and end-all when it comes to determining the worth of your selections. Any investor should understand that it will begin to lose value as soon as an option is purchased. For the option to be profitable, the underlying asset must move in the right direction with a significant delta force (ensuring that the option price will move in the same direction).

### 4.10.5 Vega

The Greek letter Vega is not a true Greek letter. Hence we don't have an illustration. Vega represents the predicted change in an option price for every percent change in implied volatility. Remember that options with high-volatility underlying assets are more costly than options with more stable underlying assets. The Vega indicator is used to indicate how variations in implied volatility might impact the price of an option.

### 4.10.6 Rho

The last Greek we'll look at is Rho, regarded as the least significant of all the Greeks21 by academics. The influence of interest rates (on US Treasury bills) on option pricing is measured by Rho. The Rho measure may be negative (for puts) or positive (for calls). Interest rates are so low that the Rho statistic is meaningless.

CHAPTER 5

# STRATEGIES FOR NEW OPTIONS TRADERS

Buying calls or put options, selling calls or put options, or both to minimize losses and achieve infinite gains are all examples of option trading strategies. Using one or more combinations to get the most feasible result depends on our criteria.

Put options offer the owner the right, but not the responsibility, to sell the underlying stock at a pre-determined price by a specific expiry period. In contrast, call options give the owner the right to acquire the underlying stock but not the obligation.

Bullish, bearish, and neutral option trading techniques may all be characterized as bullish, bearish, or neutral. Until now, it sounded intriguing? There's a little more to pique your interest.

We will show you 12 different sorts of option trading tactics that every trader should be aware of and may apply to improve their options trading game in the stock market.

## 1. Bull Call Spread

A bull call spread is a bullish options trading strategy in which one At-The-Money (ATM) call option is purchased, and the other Out-Of-The-Money call option is sold.

It's important to remember that both calls should have the same underlying stock and expiry date.

When the value of a particular stock increases, the profit is equal to the spread minus the net debit, and when the value of the commodity stock collapses, the loss is equal to the net debit. The Net Debit is the difference between the premium paid for a lower strike and the high price received for a stronger strike — the measure between the lowest and highest strike prices. When prices fall, the Bull Call Spread protects you while limiting your profit.

**Bull Spread** is a strategy achieved by combining two options of the same type, by buying an option at one strike price and selling another option at a higher strike price. This strategy may be achieved using either CALL or PUT options.

This is a limited profit / limited loss strategy, which works well in case the underlying is expected to rise moderately. This type of strategy helps to reduce the premium cost of a naked option.

Practice Exercises

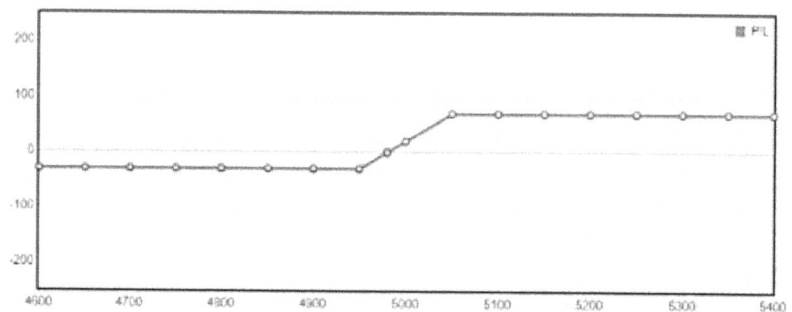

### Variables

| Description | Value |
|---|---|
| Option | ◉ Call ○ Put |
| Strike Price | 4950 |
| Gap | 100 |

### Option Transactions

| Sl | Opt | Trans | Strike | Qty | Premium |
|---|---|---|---|---|---|
| 1 | Call | Long | 4950 | 1 | 75 |
| 2 | Call | Short | 5050 | 1 | 45 |

We may conclude from the learn options example that profit and loss are capped.

When traders are not extremely bullish on a company, this approach is an excellent alternative to just purchasing a call option.

## 2. Bull Put Spread:

When options traders are somewhat positive about the underlying asset's movement, they may use this bullish options trading strategy.

Instead of purchasing calls, we purchase puts in this strategy, identical to the bull call spread. Buying one OTM Put option and selling one ITM Put option is the basis of this approach.

**Bull Spread** is a strategy achieved by combining two options of the same type, by buying an option at one strike price and selling another option at a higher strike price. This strategy may be achieved using either CALL or PUT options.

This is a limited profit / limited loss strategy, which works well in case the underlying is expected to rise moderately. This type of strategy helps to reduce the premium cost of a naked option.

Practice Exercises

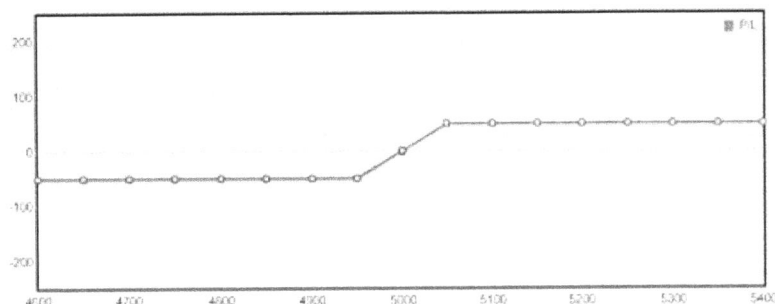

### Variables

| Description | Value |
|---|---|
| Option | ○ Call ● Put |
| Strike Price | 4950 |
| Gap | 100 |

### Option Transactions

| Sl | Opt | Trans | Strike | Qty | Premium |
|---|---|---|---|---|---|
| 1 | Put | Long | 4950 | 1 | 10 |
| 2 | Put | Short | 5050 | 1 | 60 |

It's important to remember that both puts should have the same underlying stock and expiry date.

A bull put spread is created for a net credit or net amount received, and it earns profit from a rising stock price that is limited to the net credit received. On the other hand, the potential loss is restricted when the stock price falls below the long put's strike price.

## 3. Call Ratio Back Spread:

The Call Ratio Back Spread is one of the most basic option trading methods, and it is used when a company or index is very bullish.

Traders may earn infinite gains when the market rises and restricted profits when the market falls using this method. If the market remains inside a certain range, the trader loses money. In other words, traders may earn either way as the market moves.

It is a three-legged strategy in which you purchase two OTM call options and sell one ITM call option.

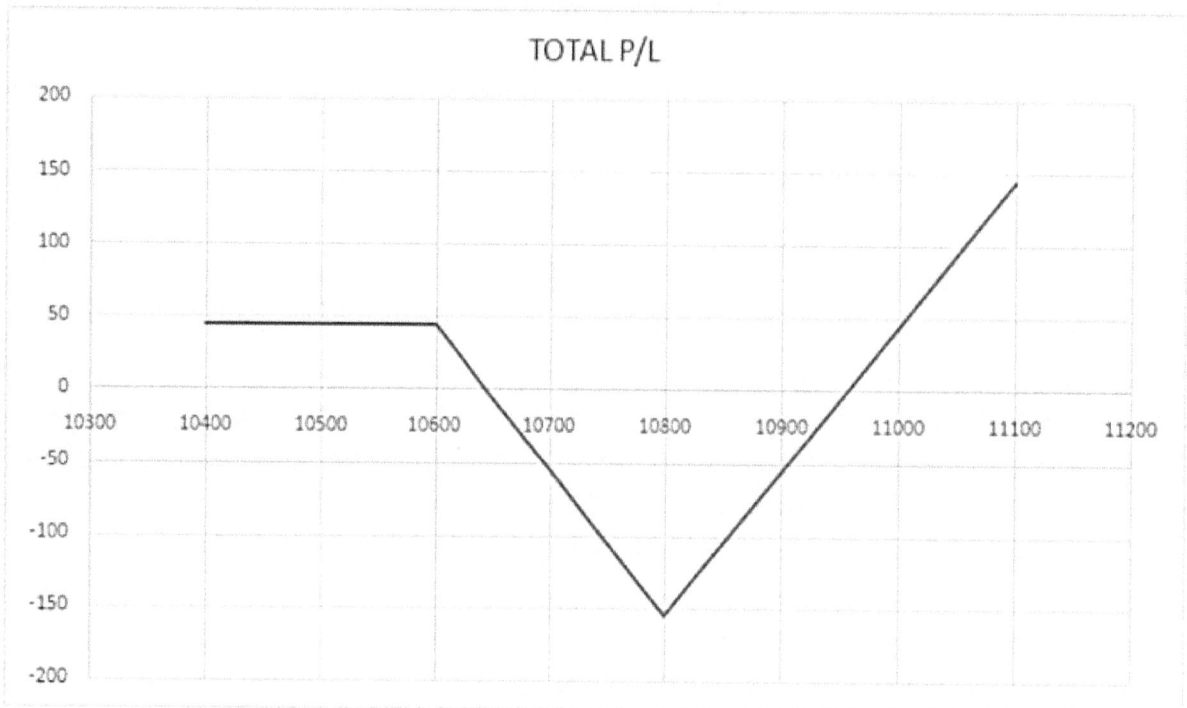

TOTAL P/L

As we can see from the P/L chart above, we earn when the price moves in either direction.

## 4. Synthetic Call:

A synthetic call is an options trading strategy employed by traders who have a long-term positive outlook of the company but are concerned about the negative risks at the same time. This method has an endless earning potential while posing a little risk.

The technique entails purchasing put options on the stock we own and on which we have a positive outlook. If the price of the underlying increases, we will benefit, but if the price falls, our loss will be restricted to the premium paid for the put option. The Protective Put options strategy is similar to this one.

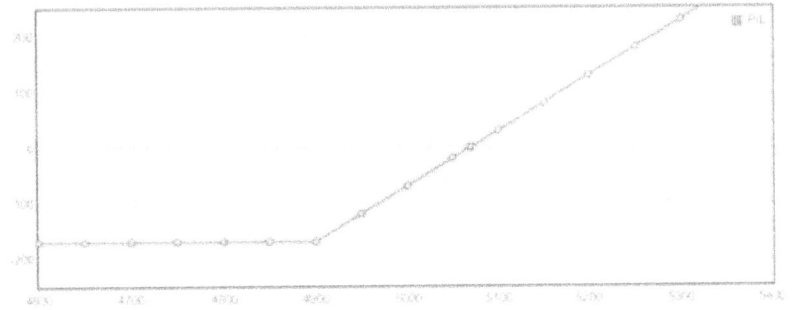

**Protective Put** is a strategy whereby a cash or Future Long position is combined with a Long Put option contract, thereby limiting the maximum loss at the cost of the premium.

Since the returns from a Protective Put are similar in nature to a Long Call option contract, this strategy is also referred to as the Synthetic Long Call.

Practice Exercises

### Variables

| Description | Value | |
|---|---|---|
| Future Price | 5000 | |
| Strike Price | 4900 | |

### Option Transactions

| Sl | Opt | Trans | Strike | Qty | Premium |
|---|---|---|---|---|---|
| 1 | Put | Long | 4900 | 1 | 70 |

### Future Transactions

| Sl | Trans | Qty | Future Price |
|---|---|---|---|
| 1 | Long | 1 | 5000 |

The risk is restricted to the premium, but the potential reward is infinite, as seen in the payout diagram above.

### 5. Bear Call Spread:

The Bear Call Spread is a two-leg option trading strategy used by options traders who have a "moderately gloomy" outlook on the market.

This technique entails purchasing one out-of-the-money call option with a higher strike price and selling one with a lower strike price. One should remember that both the calls should have the same underlying stock and the same expiry date.

A bear call spread is constructed for the net credit when the stock prices fall, and gains are gained from this method. The spread minus net credit is the maximum possible profit, whereas the maximum potential loss is the spread minus net credit. The Net Credit is calculated by subtracting the premium Paid from the premium Received.

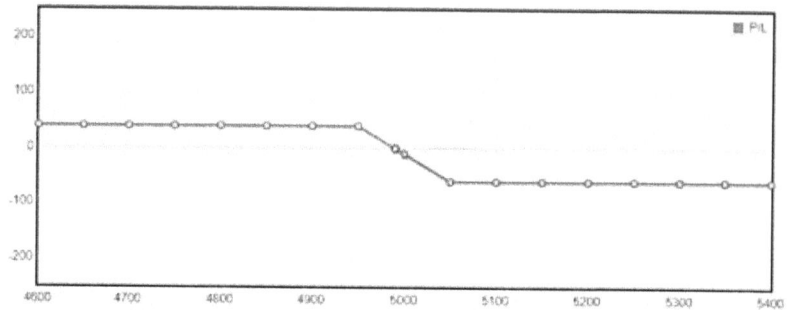

**Variables**

| Description | Value |
|---|---|
| Option | ◉ Call ○ Put |
| Strike Price | 4950 |
| Gap | 100 |

**Option Transactions**

| | SI | Opt | Trans | Strike | Qty | Premium |
|---|---|---|---|---|---|---|
| ☑ | 1 | Call | Short | 4950 | 1 | 80 |
| ☑ | 2 | Call | Long | 5050 | 1 | 40 |

As can be seen from the P/L diagram above, this approach has restricted profits equal to the net credit and limited losses equal to the spread minus the net credit.

## 6. Bear Put Spread:

The Bear Put Spread is similar to the Bull Call Spread in that it is simple to execute. When traders have a modestly pessimistic view of the market, i.e., they would use this approach when they anticipate the market to go down but not too far.

Buying the ITM Put option and selling the OTM Put option is part of this approach. It's important to remember that both puts should have the same underlying stock and expiry date. As the underlying stock declines in price, this strategy is developed for a net debit or net cost and profit.

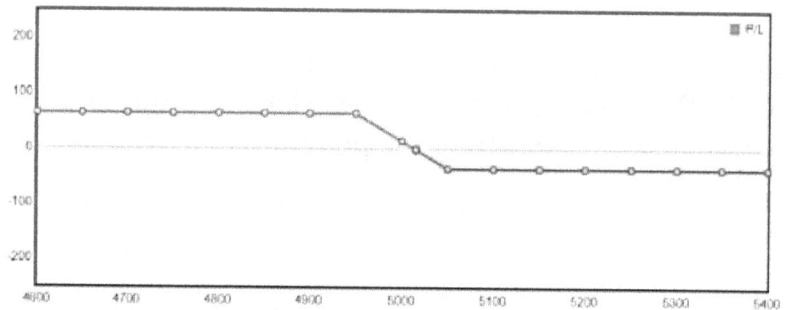

**Variables**

| Description | Value |
|---|---|
| Option | ○ Call ◉ Put |
| Strike Price | 4950 |
| Gap | 100 |

**Option Transactions**

| | SI | Opt | Trans | Strike | Qty | Premium |
|---|---|---|---|---|---|---|
| ☑ | 1 | Put | Short | 4950 | 1 | 55 |
| ☑ | 2 | Put | Long | 5050 | 1 | 90 |

The diagram shows that the profit is restricted and equal to the spread minus the net debit, and the loss is equal to the net debit. The Net Debit is calculated by subtracting the premium Paid from the premium Received.

## 7. Strip:

A strip is a bearish options strategy that entails purchasing one ATM Call and two ATM Puts.

It's important to remember that these options should all be purchased on the same underlying, with the same strike price and expiration date.

Traders may benefit when the underlying stock price makes a significant shift in either direction at the time of expiry, but in general, enormous gains are made when prices go down.

**Strip** is a strategy created by buying or selling one Call option contract and two Put Option contracts at the same strike price.

A Long strip is a more bearish approach as compared to a Long Strangle as two Put option contracts are used instead of one.

Practice Exercises

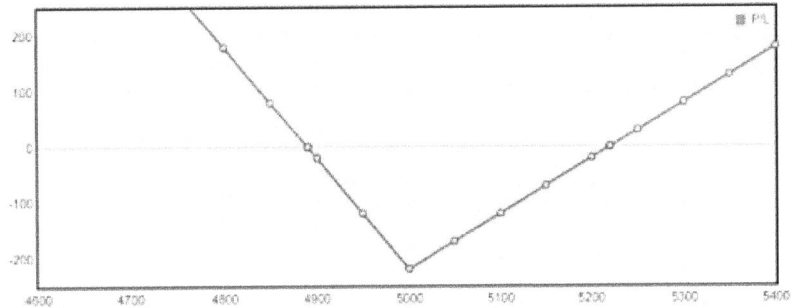

### Variables

| Description | Value |
|---|---|
| Type | ● Long ○ Short |
| Strike Price | 5000 |

### Option Transactions

| Sl | 😊 | Trans | Strike | Qty | Premium | |
|---|---|---|---|---|---|---|
| ☑ | 1 | Call | Long | 5000 | 1 | 60 |
| ☑ | 2 | Put | Long | 5000 | 2 | 80 |

The maximum profit is infinite, while the total loss associated with this approach is restricted to the net premium paid, as shown in the example above.

## 8. Synthetic Put:

A synthetic put is an options trading strategy used when investors have a pessimistic opinion of a company and are worried about the firm's possible near-term strength.

The benefit from this strategy is earned when the underlying stock price falls, which is why it's also known as the long synthetic put.

The long synthetic put gets its name because it has the same profit potential as a traditional long put.

**Long Synthetic Put** is a strategy whereby a Future Short position is combined with a Long Call option contract, thereby limiting the maximum loss at the cost of the premium.

Since the returns from this strategy are similar in nature to a Long Put option contract, this strategy is referred to as Long Synthetic Put.

Practice Exercises

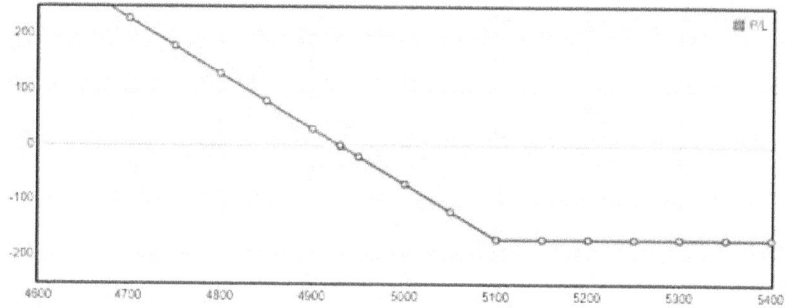

## Variables

| Description | Value |
|---|---|
| Future Price | 5000 |
| Strike Price | 5100 |

## Option Transactions

| | Sl | Opt | Trans | Strike | Qty | Premium |
|---|---|---|---|---|---|---|
| ☑ | 1 | Call | Long | 5100 | 1 | 70 |

## Future Transactions

| | Sl | Trans | Qty | Future Price |
|---|---|---|---|---|
| ☑ | 1 | Short | 1 | 5000 |

We can see from the previous example that the maximum profit and maximum loss are both infinite.

### 9. Long & Short Straddles:

The long straddle is one of the most straightforward market-neutral option trading techniques to employ, and its P&L is unaffected by market direction.

Buying ATM Call and Put options is part of this technique. It's important to remember that both options must be based on the same underlying, have the same expiration, and be in the same strike.

**Stradle** is a strategy achieved by combining a CALL and a PUT option at the same strike price. The strategy may be achieved by either going LONG in both the transactions or going SHORT in both the transactions.

A Long Stradle is favourable when the price is expected to move in either direction and it may fetch unlimited* profits, whereas the maximum loss is limited. A Short Stradle fetches profit where the expected movement in price is small.

Practice Exercises

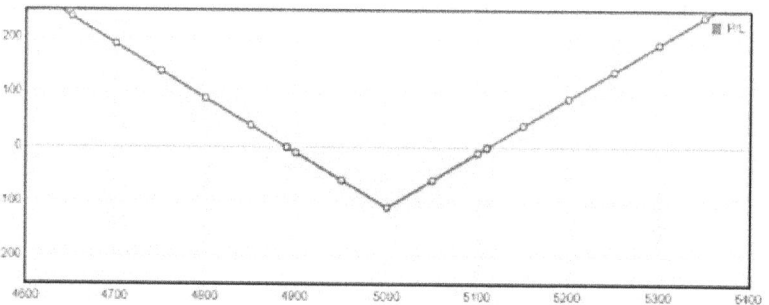

## Variables

| Description | Value |
|---|---|
| Type | ● Long  ○ Short |
| Strike Price | 5000 |

## Option Transactions

| | Sl | Opt | Trans | Strike | Qty | Premium |
|---|---|---|---|---|---|---|
| ☑ | 1 | Call | Long | 5000 | 1 | 70 |
| ☑ | 2 | Put | Long | 5000 | 1 | 40 |

Profits are boundless while losses are limited, as seen in the above graphic.

In contrast to Long Straddle, Short Straddle entails selling the ATM Call and Put option. As illustrated below, the profit is equal to the whole premium received, while the maximum loss is unlimited:

Stradle is a strategy achieved by combining a CALL and a PUT option at the same strike price. The strategy may be achieved by either going LONG in both the transactions or going SHORT in both the transactions.

A Long Stradle is favourable when the price is expected to move in either direction and it may fetch unlimited profits, whereas the maximum loss is limited. A Short Stradle fetches profit where the expected movement in price is small.

Practice Exercises

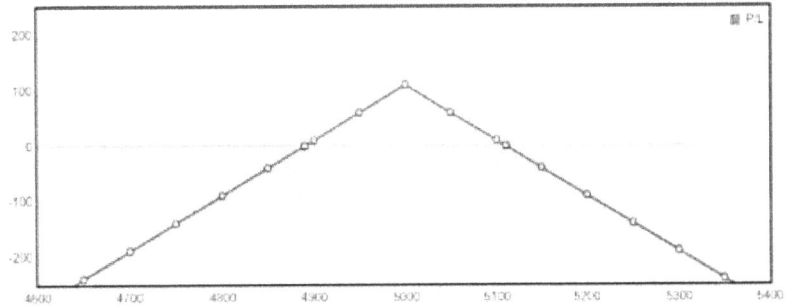

### Variables

| Description | Value |
|---|---|
| Type | ○ Long  ● Short |
| Strike Price | 5000 |

### Option Transactions

| Sl | Opt | Trans | Strike | Qty | Premium |
|---|---|---|---|---|---|
| ☑ 1 | Call | Short | 5000 | 1 | 70 |
| ☑ 2 | Put | Short | 5000 | 1 | 40 |

## 10. Long and Short Strangles:

The strangle is similar to the straddle, but the only difference is that in a straddle, we must purchase a call and put options at the ATM strike price, but in a strangle, we must buy call and put options at the OTM strike price.

One OTM put and one OTM call option are purchased in a Long Strangle. Profit is limitless in this case, while the maximum loss equals the net premium flow.

Strangle is a strategy achieved by combining a PUT option transaction with a similar CALL option transaction at a higher strike price.

A Long Strangle is favourable when the price is expected to move substantially in either direction. A short strangle is expected to fetch profits if the prices do not move too much in either direction.

Practice Exercises

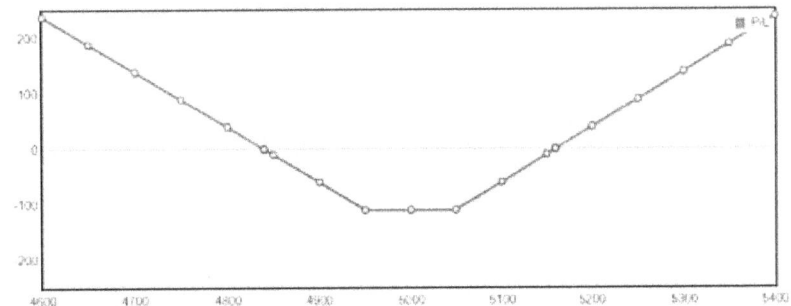

### Variables

| Description | Value |
|---|---|
| Type | ● Long  ○ Short |
| Strike Price | 4950 |
| Gap | 100 |

### Option Transactions

| Sl | Opt | Trans | Strike | Qty | Premium |
|---|---|---|---|---|---|
| ☑ 1 | Put | Long | 4950 | 1 | 70 |
| ☑ 2 | Call | Long | 5050 | 1 | 40 |

On the other hand, the Short Strangle entails selling both put and call OTM options. The maximum loss is infinite as the price increases or decreases, and the maximum profit is equal to the whole premium collected, as seen in the example below.

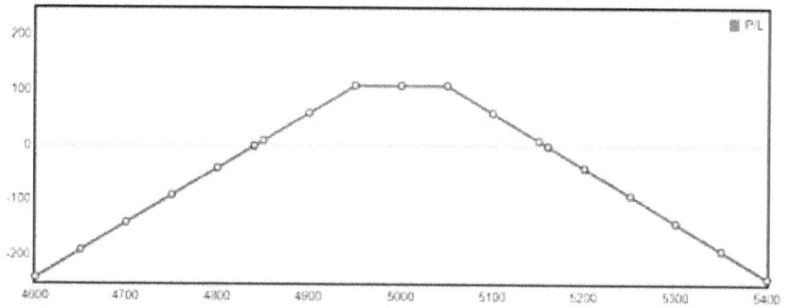

### Variables

| Description | Value |
|---|---|
| Type | ○ Long  ◉ Short |
| Strike Price | 4950 |
| Gap | 100 |

### Option Transactions

| | Sl | Opt | Trans | Strike | Qty | Premium |
|---|---|---|---|---|---|---|
| ☑ | 1 | Put | Short | 4950 | 1 | 70 |
| ☑ | 2 | Call | Short | 5050 | 1 | 40 |

## 11. Long & Short Butterfly Spread:

A butterfly spread is a neutral options trading strategy that combines bull and bear spreads with a defined risk and profit limit. The spacing between the at-the-money options is the same for options with higher and lower strike prices.

The long butterfly call spread comprises purchasing a single ITM call option, publishing two ATM call options, and obtaining one OTM call option.

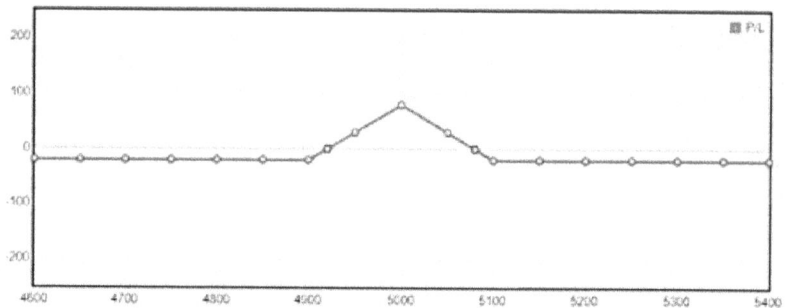

### Variables

| Description | Value |
|---|---|
| Type | ◉ Long  ○ Short |
| Option | ◉ Call  ○ Put |
| Strike Price | 5000 |
| Gap | 100 |

### Option Transactions

| | Sl | Opt | Trans | Strike | Qty | Premium |
|---|---|---|---|---|---|---|
| ☑ | 1 | Call | Long | 4900 | 1 | 70 |
| ☑ | 2 | Call | Short | 5000 | 2 | 40 |
| ☑ | 3 | Call | Long | 5100 | 1 | 30 |

Selling one in-the-money call option, purchasing two at-the-money call options, and selling one out-of-the-money call option is the short butterfly spread strategy.

Butterfly Spread is achieved by combining a Bull Spread and a Bear Spread. It is a limited risk, non-directional options strategy that is designed to have a large probability of earning a limited profit.

For a Long butterfly, the trader sells two option contracts at the middle strike price and buys one option contract at a lower strike price and one option contract at a higher strike price. Either puts or calls can be used for a butterfly spread.

Practice Exercises

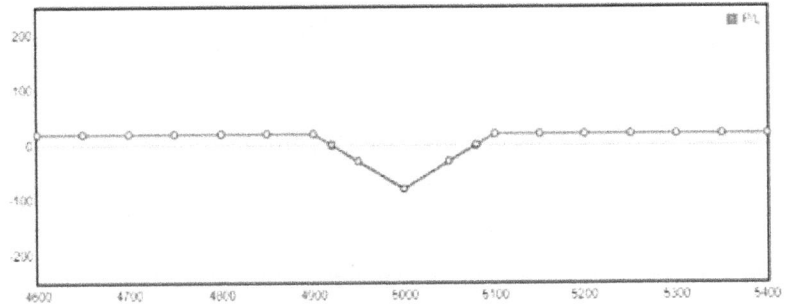

### Variables

| Description | Value |
|---|---|
| Type | ○ Long ● Short |
| Option | ● Call ○ Put |
| Strike Price | 5000 |
| Gap | 100 |

### Option Transactions

| | Sl | Opt | Trans | Strike | Qty | Premium |
|---|---|---|---|---|---|---|
| ☑ | 1 | Call | Short | 4900 | 1 | 70 |
| ☑ | 2 | Call | Long | 5000 | 2 | 40 |
| ☑ | 3 | Call | Short | 5100 | 1 | 30 |

## 12. Long and Short Iron Condor:

An iron condor is a four-stroke option trading strategy that consists of two puts (one long and one short) and two calls (one long and one short). The expiry dates must all be the same.

Iron Condor is a non-directional strategy that has limited risk and offers limited maximum profits. It is similar to the Condor but is created using two Call and two Put option contracts, unlike the Condor which is created using all Call or all Put option contracts.

For an iron condor, the trader buys or sells a Strangle at the two middle strike price and sells or buys another strangle using lower and higher strike prices.

Practice Exercises

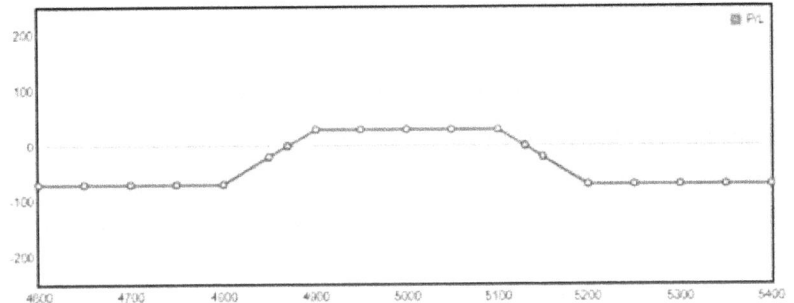

### Variables

| Description | Value |
|---|---|
| Type | ● Long ○ Short |
| Strike Price | 4800 |
| Gap | 100 |
| 2nd Gap | 200 |

### Option Transactions

| | Sl | Opt | Trans | Strike | Qty | Premium |
|---|---|---|---|---|---|---|
| ☑ | 1 | Put | Long | 4800 | 1 | 70 |
| ☑ | 2 | Put | Short | 4900 | 1 | 60 |
| ☑ | 3 | Call | Short | 5100 | 1 | 50 |
| ☑ | 4 | Call | Long | 5200 | 1 | 10 |

The maximum profit is generated when the underlying stock implodes between the middle valuations at expiration.

# 5.1 Tips for Success for Beginners

### 5.1.1 Recognize when it's time to change your strategy

While having a strategy is critical in options trading, recognizing when your project needs improvement is also critical. Even though your emotions urge you to adhere to your plan, there will be occasions when you must deviate from it. When a trader's aim no longer applies to the present scenario, they are successful. Having a plan establishes your course, but it does not imply that you would mindlessly follow it until the end of the earth.

Every trader reaches a time when something beyond their control occurs, rendering their strategy ineffective in that scenario.

That is why, while making a strategy, be aware of its flaws and potential for failure. Market circumstances are always changing, so what is true now may not be true tomorrow. So, if you're thinking of sticking to your preset course of action even though market circumstances have shifted 180 degrees, you're making a huge error. You will only fail as a result of it. Yes, understanding your emotions, overcoming obstacles, and changing conditions will take much work. However, any modest move in the right direction, including awareness of the imbalance, is progress.

### 5.1.2 Before you begin, be sure you have a plan for your exit and entry

One of the most important skills to master is determining the best entry and exit points for options trading. Nothing, no matter how brilliant you're adjusting skills are, can make up for a bad entrance, and you might wind up losing a lot of money as a result.

However, something much more crucial than learning to establish the proper entrance and exit locations. Are you able to figure out what it is? Recognize that you must practice your entrance and exit points before the money is removed from the table. New options traders believe that every transaction must result in massive profits, and they need every penny of it. However, it would help if you broke away from this mindset. It might be a significant barrier for any novice trader.

As long as you have a sound and lucrative trading strategy, you will earn from multiple deals in the future. Sticking to just one of them as if it were the final deal you'll ever make is a bad idea that will only result in a loss.

So, don't be concerned about those modest additional earnings; you've already earned a certain amount of profit from the deal, and now you need to secure it. Yes, ignoring this advice and continuing with your trading attitude may result in a few more dollars here and there, but the chances are that the loss will outweigh the gain. You'll wind up losing all of your profits before ever having a chance to pull the trigger.

### 5.1.3 Trades that aren't in the money should be avoided

A few tactics may help you earn on out-of-the-money call options, but they are the exception. You could be drawn to out-of-the-money call options as a beginning investor in options trading since they are reasonable and cheap. Even so, you should keep in mind that the stock market and the options market are two distinct circumstances.

Even if you look at the underlying equities to purchase the options, buying cheap and selling high is not a practical strategy. If a call has gone out-of-the-money, it has a little possibility of rising to the requisite levels before its expiry date. If you continue to purchase these options, you are essentially gambling with your money.

### 5.1.4 Don't Reduce the Size of Your Homework

There are several examples of options traders losing money simply because they did not study. If you question novice traders, they will almost always admit not completing thorough market research. They don't even do their homework before making a transaction. Do you understand why I'm so concerned about doing your assignment correctly? If you don't, you'll never be aware of the data release dates, seasonal trends, or trading patterns that expert traders are aware of. New traders are so enthralled by the prospect of executing a transaction as quickly as possible that they overlook the need to do research, which turns out to be a costly lesson for them.

Even if you are not interested in investing, you should study it. When you do extensive study, you will learn everything about a certain financial statement and be completely aware of your road. If you intend to invest in options, you must first learn about the different tactics available.

Remember that every other trader has access to the same information as you, so if you put out the effort, you can even discover the assets that will produce high returns.

You should also make a weekly commitment to yourself to read at least one new book on options trading. Reading books teaches you numerous secrets and introduces you to new ideas. You'll also have a better understanding of the benefits and drawbacks of options trading.

### 5.1.5 Instead of trading for wealth, trade for income

You should rethink if you believe that options trading would provide you with up to 150 percent returns. Yes, some investments can provide you with such amounts now and again, but not every transaction is like that. Most novice traders believe that trading options will make them rich immediately, but this is not the case.

If you think you're doing options trading to make money, you're mistaken. It's more like figuring out the best way to earn a consistent income. If you're eager for more money, you'll be more inclined to ignore the dangerous ventures and put your money into them regardless. Remember that options trading is fraught with dangers, so proceed with caution.

### 5.1.6 Never trust unsubstantiated advice

Another common mistake made by rookie traders is trusting in random advice. Almost every trader makes this error at some time throughout their career. It's possible that one of your friends or family has been talking about a certain firm whose stocks are doing well, and they're hoping to earn a huge profit by investing in that stock. Before you believe anything, you should do your homework. I'm not claiming that what they're saying is incorrect. It might be accurate, but that doesn't mean you have to jump on it right away, as if it's the next great thing, and you'll lose it if you don't act quickly. Before you hurry to your online brokerage right now, take a step back and conduct some research. The example given above is only one example of a source of false information.

Another source is television and social media. On both of these platforms, you'll often discover investing pros who can't stop raving about a certain stock as if it's a must-have investment. Even yet, if you dig far enough into the subject, you'll discover that it's nothing out of the norm. You must remember that trading is nothing more than a speculative bet if you continue to follow media suggestions.

But just because there's a lot of chatter about false information doesn't mean you should disregard everything you hear. If something has attracted your interest and you can't seem to let go of it, you should first consider if the source is trustworthy. The next step is to do your homework, which will provide you with the necessary knowledge. As a result, don't depend on others to tell you what to do. You must choose whether or not it is the appropriate form of investment for you. You may also get a second opinion from someone trustworthy and neutral.

### 5.1.7 Begin with Enough Funding

Although you do not need much cash to start, you should have enough to get your business up and running. In layman's words, wealth is the amount of money you should have in your trading account to cover any transaction costs, and this same capital will also protect you if you lose money while trading.

You should always have some money in your trading account.

When making trades, you should not be concerned about financial transfers, and the fact that the money is already in your account suggests that everything will go well. Your broker can also assist you without causing any delays in transferring funds. If you ask the market's most successful traders, they will all say the same thing. They constantly retain some money in their account and check it from time to time to ensure that even if they make a few bad deals in the future, the money in the report will serve as a cushion.

### 5.1.8 Don't buy too much with your margin

The term margin was defined at the start of this book. It occurs when you borrow money from your broker to acquire options. In certain circumstances, margins may help you earn more money; but if you lose money, the losses will become much more accentuated due to the margins. As a result, you must have a thorough grasp of how margin operates. You should also be aware that utilizing margins implies your broker may ask you to sell your options at any moment.

New traders are prone to get carried away because they believe margins equate to free money, so they continue to utilize them until the nightmare arrives. Assume you've employed margin, but the investment has now deteriorated.

It implies you owe the broker a significant amount of money for nothing since you did not make any gains. It's analogous to purchasing alternatives with a credit card. Would you do anything like that? Isn't that correct? When you utilize margins excessively, it's the same thing.

# 5.2 Mistakes to Avoid when Trading

### 5.2.1 Getting Into a Trade That Is Too Big

One of the most common errors individuals make is taking on too many positions in options trading. People aren't accustomed to investing in tiny sums since our options aren't very expensive compared to stock pricing.

Even those who are not wealthy consider the stock market and how much 100 shares cost. This concept has the potential to get individuals into trouble. If you have the funds to buy or sell contracts, you may be tempted to move on a big number of them when you first start trading. It has the potential to get individuals into trouble. It's not about the money; it's about being in a position where you're not prepared to respond as swiftly as you may need to depend on the scenario. So, if you discover trade and decide to sell 20 futures, attempting to purchase those 20 contracts back if the firm fails might be difficult. Alternatively, you may find yourself purchasing many call options and having problems getting rid of them on the same day. It's preferable to have a few distinct tiny positions with alternatives rather than a vast number of diverse functions. Keep in mind that option pricing change often. You don't want to over-leverage your transactions and find yourself in a situation where you can't sell all 10 or 20 contracts.

### 5.2.2 Paying No Attention to the Expiration Date

It is perhaps one of the most typical blunders made by inexperienced traders. As you submit your trades, we consider the expiry date one of the most important considerations. And after you've started a company, you'll need to have the choices' expiry dates tattooed on your forehead. It's not something that can simply be disregarded. First and foremost, when initiating a position, selecting the expiry date is just as crucial as selecting the option's strike price. A novice must place an excessive amount of emphasis on the opportunity's pricing and the strike's price-setting. The opportunity cost and the strike price are critical, as is the expiry date.

### 5.2.3 Purchasing Low-Cost Alternatives

You get what you paid for, as the phrase goes. There are occasions when buying out of the money options makes sense, but you shouldn't go too far. Unfortunately, many new traders succumb to the temptation of trading far out of the money to purchase a low-cost option. The issue with these options is that they may generate money even if they are out of money. They're not going to see any activity if they're too far out of the money. So there's no point in purchasing a low-cost alternative simply because it's just $25. You don't want to put your money into options where a large price change is required to make any money.

It's reasonable to invest in options that are close to the money. Even if they are out of money, opportunities close to being in the money may be highly beneficial.

So, if you're seeking to save a little money when you first start investing, that's something to think about. However, to earn money, the fundamental criterion is that there must be a real likelihood that the stock prices will change enough to make the option you purchased profitable.

### 5.2.4 Failure to close is a big no-no when it comes to selling options

If there's one thing you remember from our discussion of selling options, whether it's selling put credit spreads or naked puts, bear in mind that you may always quit the deal. When you sell to open, you purchase to close, which is how you quit your job. You should be cautious about this since it's all too easy to give in to your emotions and fear and abandon a transaction prematurely. However, you must be mindful of the prospect of having to liquidate the company at any point. Riding out an option until it expires is a bad idea unless it's clear that it'll expire out of the money.

As a result of this issue, novice options traders often enter the market with a home-based approach. Hope isn't a strategy when it comes to investing. The word "hope" is associated with casino slot machine games.

When considering your training alternatives, you should make the most sensible selection possible given the conditions. So, as the expiry date approaches and you know the trade will not be lucrative, resist the urge to wait for a trend reversal.

It is the worst of all potential methods for individuals purchasing options to open positions. Remember that time is always working against you when buying to open a component. There is no need to retain the option unless the stock is trending in the correct direction. Time decay works to your advantage as a seller. However, there are times when leaving the trade is the best option.

Let's have a look at a few instances.

If you sell to open an iron condor and the stock breaks out in one way or the other for any reason, it's best to exit the iron condor immediately. We're not talking about a one-dollar or two-dollar bill here. If the market moves in such a way that one of your options ends up in the money by a little margin, it's worth waiting to see what happens.

It would be stupid to persist in the trade if there is a significant break to the upside or negative. For one thing, you'd be in danger of being assigned, but the most probable scenario is that you'd lose the most money possible.

However, suppose you have a strong strategy and only invest in options with much open interest. In that case, you should be able to purchase and sell that option very rapidly, regardless of the scenario.

### 5.2.5 Investing in Illiquid Options

I'm going to repeat this word since it's so vital. When trading options, liquidity is crucial. Liquidity refers to the capacity to promptly acquire and sell financial assets and convert them to cash. It isn't enough to like a firm to begin trading options on it. If the open interest for a vote is merely 8, 10, or even 45 percent, you'll run into problems if you need to get rid of an option quickly. Liquid choices are usually available at the major firms, but you should always double-check. Liquid index funds are also available. Any company with a tiny open interest should be avoided. When the real component is little, the only way to trade is if the risk of losing money on the deal is negligible. So, in addition to the strike price, share price, and expiry date, you should pay particular attention to open interest. You don't want to get yourself in a position where you can't get out.

### 5.2.6 Lacking a Trading Strategy

One of the nicest aspects of options trading is how simple it is. So you have this low-cost opportunity to get into the stock market, and it's also quite simple to handle on your own. These are all wonderful aspects. However, there is a drawback. The disadvantage is that it is so simple that people start trading on a whim. Don't get me wrong: just because it's simple doesn't mean the stakes or possible losses aren't serious. As a result, you must take this very seriously. Spend some time developing a trading strategy. Many of the topics we discussed before, such as the degree of profit you're ready to take on every transaction, should be included in your trading strategy. It should also specify a limit for when you should depart your positions. But there's one thing I failed to say. When trading options, your trading strategy should also include a maximum of five financial instruments on which you will concentrate your efforts. Doing more than five financial assurances, in my view, is more than your mind can manage. You should be keeping a careful eye on each of the firms for whom you were exchanging index funds. That isn't going to work if you have more than five.

And as I've previously said, one of the characteristics of options trading is that prices may fluctuate extremely fast.

So, if you attempt to focus your attention in 20 different ways, you'll almost certainly lose money since you won't be able to keep up with everything.

Your trading strategy should also involve some variety. When choosing the five stocks you'll use to trade your options the next year, avoid selecting assets from the same sector. You may choose a few from the same industry, but make sure they're not the same.

# AFTERWORD

Options trading has been practiced for thousands of years in some form or another. All of the fundamentals for effective options trading that you've studied here (and will learn elsewhere) aren't confined to equities. Options trading is available on the CBOE and other exchanges for various instruments, including currencies, exchange-traded funds, mutual funds, futures, commodities, and more. If you have a good understanding of the markets in any of these sectors, you'll be able to utilize what you've learned in the options market.

Always do your homework before investing, regardless matter how big or little it is. It is necessary to do research. It's what will help you make the best investing selection possible. "Knowledge is power," as the adage goes. The more you know about something, the better you'll forecast how it will do in the market. That is why research is so important. It will enable you to determine if something is worthwhile to invest in. Keep in mind that you're working with a constantly changing market; therefore, it's only natural that you keep up with the newest advances and changes. Doing research is one approach to do this.

Writing a diary may be useful, even if it is not required. To write a memoir, you do not need to be a professional writer; nonetheless, you must accomplish two things: Regularly update your diary and be honest with whatever you write about it. You will be able to more effectively recognize your strengths and flaws if you keep a notebook. It may also assist you in recognizing lessons that you would otherwise miss.

It is usually a good idea to prepare ahead of time, whether you are about to start forex trading or trading in general. Make sure you have a clear direction in mind. It's also a great strategy to keep your emotions in check and prevent greed. You should have both a short-term and long-term strategy. You should also be prepared for any eventuality. Of course, it is difficult to anticipate every eventuality. If you find yourself in an unexpected and difficult circumstance, take your time to investigate the issue and devise a fresh strategy.

Never take action without first making a thorough strategy. Poor preparation leads to poor execution, while a brilliant concept almost always pays off. You should adhere to your to-do list. However, there are times when you may need to leave your project, such as when you discover that continuing to the same program will not provide the desired results or when you come up with a superior concept. Proper planning may provide you with a sense of direction and guarantee that your execution is successful.

www.ingramcontent.com/pod-product-compliance
Lightning Source LLC
Chambersburg PA
CBHW081823200326
41597CB00023B/4362